The Vagrant Shadow

Feral Nation #1

DEDICATION

I would like to dedicate this book to my Family Members who never stopped
believing in me: Mom, Dad, Tom, Kelley, Erin, Juan, Mark, Carmen, David,
Kathy, Julie, Erika, Nate, Uncle Mike, Aunt Donna, Michelle, Grandpa Tom,
Grandma Mildred, Uncle Neal, Matt, Steve, and Aunt Betty.
I would also like to dedicate this book to those of you who are reading this
book, Thank You

Message from Daniel

I would like to personally thank you for picking this book to read. It is my first book I have ever written and I am very proud of how it turned out. Creating Thomas was such a thrill to me, I hope you find the book an exciting read just as I have found it exciting to write. Once again, I thank you and hope you enjoy the story.

DANIEL DEMBSKI PRESENTS:

THE VAGRANT SHADOW

PRELUDE

Night—the darkness enveloped me like a cobra envelopes its prey.

With each passing minute, the night grew colder, and cobra grew hungrier. Calculating the predicament I was in, I would assume that the dampness made the air seem fifty degrees if not cooler. As I lay on the cold, hard ground my body began to shiver; the cobra has begun its feast.

They say that we fear what we do not understand, which I believe is true. My fear of the unknown grew in me, and the longer I stayed, the more fear enveloped my being. I couldn't leave the shelter—not during the night at least....but I had to, the cave was becoming gloomier, and hazier just like my memory of how I got here. The night air draped around me like it was nurturing me with by its blanket of death. As I huddled my knees together, feeling the goose bumps on my skin creep as a violent shiver went down my spine; an eerie and ominous howl of the wolfs lament has caught up to me—the pack must have caught wind of my whereabouts as the howl resonated through the storm, it shattered the only peace of mind I had left, leaving me vulnerable for the cobra to digest.

We left that bitter state of Wisconsin behind in the middle of February for my Aunt Flora's wedding. As mom and I boarded the plane, we were disappointed to find that we were separated, so instead of sitting next to my mom, I got to sit next to some sleazebag with excessive body odor and some sort of respiratory condition. He looked like he was in the thirties, but judging by his poor hygiene, I assumed he was unemployed and lived in the basement of his parents. I pulled out the *Sky Mall* magazine from the pouch and flipped through it lazily while the flight attendant gave the usual mandatory safety precautions. The man next to me wouldn't stop coughing and it seemed like his asthma was acting up; frankly I was getting rather annoyed by him. Rolling my eyes as I looked back over the seat and caught my mom's eye she waved to me with an innocent wave. *"Help me"*, my eyes pleaded. My mother sighed and shook her head. Her actions spoke *"Sorry."* I leaned back in my chair and closed my eyes. The man's disruptive breathing kept me from falling asleep so I put in my head phones on. The wave of music soothed my nervous acrophobia as we sailed smoothly into the clouded atmosphere.

I was quickly awakened by the sudden jerk of a forward motion as my stomach lurched into my tightened seat belt. My weary eyes adjusted to the cabins lighted atmosphere as the captain came on the intercom.

"Good evening passengers and welcome to Elkton Oregon. This is your captain speaking. I would like to thank you for flying with us today; it's a little breezy with a high of 60 degrees expected. Please put your tray away and place your seat in the upright position our flight crew will be coming around to collect your garbage, please remained seated until the seatbelt light has been turned off, and we hope that you have enjoyed your flight. Thanks again for flying Frontier Airlines and have a great evening," When we landed, I remained in my seat while everyone clamored to get their luggage from the overhead compartments Then, as I was about to leave, the man next to me began to talk. I rolled my eyes and sighed silently answering minimal questions as possible.

"So where are you from?" he asked.

"Wisconsin," I replied.

"Oh, how do you like it there?"

"I don't."

"Why is that?"

"There is nothing there except dirt and cows,"

"Oh, that's too bad. I am from Ohio,"

"Sounds nice," I mumbled.

"It's alright; a lot of history there. I am actually heading to a wedding, my sister is getting married,"

"Have fun." I said and just then my mother thankfully appeared and I was finally able to get my luggage.

"Well, hey it was nice talking to you," the man said as he stuck out his hand. I looked at his hand, and shook it quickly. The feeling of grease sticking to my palm made me shudder with disgust. My mom glanced at the man, then at me, and smiled.

"Are you ready?" she asked. I held on to the handle of my suitcase in front of me, elbows in trying to maneuver through the narrow aisle, ignoring the man as much as possible. I walked slowly and sullenly down the carpeted airport, a twinge of fear shot down my spine as I viciously dug through my pockets, feeling nothing but lint and empty air. My mom stopped and looked at me.

"What is it?" she asked.

"My iPod, I think I left it on the plane," She groaned "Ohhh...Thomas," she began, "wherever it is, it's probably gone now." The words hit me like an arrow to the heart. I began to walk down the airport hallway with my suitcase grasped tightly in my right hand. The weight of the luggage seemed to weigh down my arm as it banged awkwardly against my thigh with each step I took. Mom looked at me out of the corner of her eye and shook her head. As I glanced up at the escalator sign, there was a familiar raspy voice-the asthmatic sleazebag. I turned around as he waved his hand, coughing with each step he took. I was surprised that he could still walk. He caught up to my mother and me and coughed into his sleeve.

"Hey, I believe this belongs to you," he said opening his hand to reveal an iPod.

"You dropped it while you were getting your bag out," I looked at him in disbelief as he handed it over.

"I don't know what to say," I said a little shocked but very happy.

"Maybe *Thank You*?" my mom sneered at me, "I shouldn't have to tell you that." I smiled gratefully at the man.

"Thanks." The man walked about fifty feet away when I overhead him talking on the phone with someone:

"Hey Flora, I just flew in, the flight was pretty long, I had to sit next to some brat that was exceptionally rude; but other than that, there weren't to many delays, I am actually heading up to my hotel soon, when should I meet you and Gene for dinner?" There was a tightening in my gut as the sound of the man's voice faded into the chatter of the anxious passengers as we walked into the cool night air. The cab pulled up to the curb just as we walked out of the airport terminal the driver jumped out to help us with our luggage. The street lamps accelerated into a blur as the cab drove us to the hotel. Both of us were exhausted from the flight. We pulled into a nice drive way that had a round-about with a statue and water fountain set in the center. Lights illuminated the fountain with pale hues of reds and greens. Upon entering the elegant atmosphere, we were greeted by the attendant who stood behind the front desk. After a few moments of exchanging information, we headed down a lit up sophisticated hallway adorned with floral wallpaper and lovely scenic paintings. The hotel room was cold, the air conditioner was set at 66 degrees and running. The air smelled like fresh linen. We sat our bags down each on our own bed, as I cranked up the heat to about 70 degrees. I quickly got dressed as my mom went into the bathroom. Plopping on the bed and resting my head against the pillows was like heaven. A contemplated sigh erupted from my chest as my body began to relax. It wasn't before long that the sun peeped through the window as my mom shook me awake. Opening my eyes slowly, I yawned and stretched planting my feet on the carpeting she had turned on the T.V. and the morning news came into my undivided attention. She was heading to breakfast: *did I want to come?* Without waiting for a reply, she clicked off the television and headed down to the lobby, leaving me alone in the room.

The steady rhythmic beads of the hot shower trickled down my pale skin as thoughts seemed to be emerging from my unconscious mind. I couldn't stop thinking about my brother and what he would be doing if he was alive. I could still see his face—tan and handsome, his black hair waving through the wind as he turned around to face me as he smiled. Ever since the freak accident, I really haven't been able to overcome the feeling of dread: he was only 16 when his brakes failed during the middle of turn on a yellow light; some idiot wasn't paying attention and T-boned him—the impact killed him instantly. I closed my eyes and let the warm water rush over me, as inhaled deeply. The rich steam shrouded my naked body as I could feel my heart begin to race rapidly; it pounded against my chest like a feral prime ape beating against reinforced enclosure. I looked at my hand which held a bar of soap, for some reason I couldn't quite grasp the soap as my whole left arm began to tremble. I dropped the soap, as I felt the shower spinning. The swirling mesh left me nauseous as vomited on to the tub floor. Acidic stomach components scalded my throat as I began to see double. I reached for the handle on the tub wall, but managed to miss. My feet gave way from underneath me and in my last failed attempts to grab something, I held on to the shower curtain ripping it off the bar that held it in place. My face landed on in the wet bowl, and I was knocked cold, my withdrawals had claimed me once again.

<u>Chapter 1</u>

There are two and a half men in the forest. Something sinister lurked through the dark and musty forest. I could see myself peer through the trees as I watched closely, I don't know what they were up to, but it didn't feel right one man was in a wheel chair. He seemed to be in his mid-thirties, frail frame with both his legs missing. He carried something in his hand…a gun perhaps? Did this other man who was with him have a death wish, or was it capital punishment? These thoughts seemed to be wandering through my mind as I stepped very carefully. Like a translucent spirit within the dimension of a new unfamiliar world, I stepped beside the men and observed them with interest keeping a low profile behind some foliage. The tallest man held a duffle bag that slung loosely over his shoulder while the shorter man rolled over to a spot and pointed to the ground.

"Set one right here," The shorter man instructed, "These damn bears have been eating my game. I got to feed myself too you know." The tall man unstrapped the bag from his shoulder and dropped it heavily near the shorter man who seemed to jump in response.

"Damn it, watch what you're doing! You nearly clipped my toe off!" The tall man scoffed and unzipped the bag, pulling out a bear trap from the encasement.

"Not like you have any toes to feel with," the tall man muttered silently to himself.

"What was that?" the man in the chair asked.

"Nothing, I was just talking to myself," he said under his breath. He set the trap and baited it with a rancid piece of fish, then he covered it gently with leaves, setting a stick in the dirt upright to indicate that the trap was set.

"Idiot," the short man called. "Don't do that, the bears will know it's a trap!" the taller man rolled his eyes and kept walking.

"These animals don't think like us," the shorter man snorted as kicked the taller man in the butt with his prosthetic foot.

"Don't back talk me, asshole!" he scolded. I continued to watch while the taller man set the traps as they travelled deep into the woods.

"Why did you choose Timber Falls out of all the places?"

The short man gave a glare.

"None of your business. Now shut up and help me into the jeep,"
The tall man rolled his eyes and helped elevate the short man into the
vehicle as just as the sun was beginning to set behind the thick trees. As
the jeep seemed to roll towards me, the blinding lights seemed to shimmer
right through my body and I stood there watching in horror like a deer in
the head lights. It wasn't until the jeep ran right through me, when I thrust
back into reality with a cold sweat running down my face, machinery was
hooked up to my body as the EKG beeped rhythmically. I blinked and
glanced around the room. I was in a hospital. Blinding beams of sterile
light reflected off the white walls and silver slits of the window blinds I
felt numb as I lay my head back down on the pillow trying to remember
my dream; my head swirling with confusion, just as a headache began to
form. For some reason, it was suddenly all a blur and I couldn't quite
piece together what happened. All I could remember was taking a shower,
and then waking up in the hospital. The dream was non-existent, like I
stepped into Pandora's Box of an altered reality that I was not supposed to
see. *What could this mean?* I groaned as the door swung open, my mother
storming in, shaking a bottle of white pills at me.

"Thomas Kenneth Bravier, what on earth has gotten into you? First you have been fired from your job, now you are overdosing on pills. Are you *trying* to kill yourself?" she asked in rage. I propped myself on my elbows and cocked an eyebrow. Mom's eyes bewildered with rage shook a finger at me.

"Don't you *dare* give me your cocky brows, mister, how can you do this to me, your one and *only* mother?"

I couldn't help but drone out her voice as my mind rendered into relapse and I slipped into another mini coma.

I was awoken by a gentle shake. My mind was vacant from the previous dream as I opened my blood shot eyes. I was greeted by my girlfriend's soft smile which quickly turned into a

Look of disappointment and dismay. She bit her lip, as she reached over to kiss me on the forehead.

"Anna! What are you doing here?" I questioned suspiciously. Anna gave a devious smirk.

"I came to see you, silly…*and* my grandmother is on her deathbed, so I had to come see her one last time or be taken out of the will. Anyways, how are you feeling? Any better?"

20

"Yeah I am fine, just had a panic attack," I muttered closing my eyes. Even through the darkness of my eyelids I could feel her scornful expression.

"Not just *a* panic attack," she said disdainfully. "You overdosed on my last round of ecstasy," I opened one bloodshot eye open to look at her.

"Yeah, so, I will get you another round,"

"And just how do you think that you're going to do that, hm? With what money do you *possibly* have? Your whole paycheck was blown on gambling, for crying out loud, you're fifteen *hundred* in the hole!"

I winced at her words. She was right. I had a serious problem…an addiction to everything. Here I thought I was going to Oregon for my Aunt's wedding to escape life, when in fact I was really escaping myself and my problems. The nurse came in disconnect my I.V. tube.

"Good afternoon Thomas, I have some good news. You can leave today. I need you to sign some discharge papers. Also your mother explained to us that you have been sleeping in irregular places, we ran some tests, and found out you have narcolepsy. The doctor prescribed you some medication that should *only* be taken in the presence of your mother to avoid the risk of overdose. We wouldn't want you to end up here again

21

Thomas," The nurse handed me a pen and I took it to sign my name along the dotted lines. Before long I was released from the hospital. The events that followed left me worn out and soon I found my way to my Aunt's house. I don't remember how I got there, but the next time I woke up, was probably the most disturbing thing I had ever woken up too: very heavy panting followed by rancid breath and a lick to face. I was disgruntled for being woken up at a such an ungodly hour, however what irritated me more was the fact that my aunt had allowed her fifty pound Siberian Husky into the room where he so boldly place his front paws on my shoulders while his reeking breath pierced my skin and let his lips loom over mine so that his drool dripped on to the corner of my mouth. It tasted so foul that I sat up and wiped my mouth on my arm and pushed him off my bed, throwing a slipper at him, causing him to yelp and run out of my room. Wiping my mouth from dog spit, I looked around my room, and noticed that I was not in the hospital any more, but I was in a small guest bedroom that had very few items—only the essentials: Desk, a bed, a dresser, and a night stand that held the Holy Bible and a Vitamin pamphlet. My clothes and my bag were by the door, but I noticed that my cell phone was missing. I laid back down and groaned as I pulled a pillow over my face trying to barricade the suns bright rays from reaching my

pale perplexed pigment. Nothing would make me leave the bedroom, but

for some reason I had an inkling that there was something going on. I got

up groggily and watched from the banister completely undetected. What I

was witnessing would change the perception of the way I saw Anna

forever.

Chapter 2

The grandfather clock struck noon when the doorbell rang. It was such an odd sound; the clock struck at about the same tone as the doorbell if not a little louder, but hearing those chimes synchronize at the exact moment as one another gave the house an eerie ring to it. I leaned against the banister with interest which was above the front door way. Lesli, who was my cousin's step-sister suffered from a rare disease known as Sirenomelia, (a rare disease in which legs fused together to look like a fish tail).

She sat innocently in her wheelchair. She looked so odd, yet at the same time she looked quite beautiful. Despite her lack of mobility in her legs, she had a sort of soft aurora around her and a strong personality to go with—just like I remember when we were kids.

The sun shone brightly against her rich blond hair as her frame was illuminated—almost like a holy radiance had enveloped her being. I couldn't quite help but stare at her before I turned my attention to Max who was barking quite gruffly at the stranger, wagging his tail wildly. I couldn't see who he was greeting but I could tell by the clipping of his nails against the hickory hard wood flooring that he was doing his happy prance. When Max met a stranger, his behavior is quite peculiar: he would

first bound to the door, bark once, sniff the mail slot, and then bark again

before sitting at door waiting. When the strange entered the home, he

would circle them once, nudge their pocket for any food, then go lay down

which usually resulted

in very loud snoring to follow. A familiar voice came into ear shot my

head quickly turned in shock.

"I am sorry to bother you ma'am my name is Anna, I am Thomas'

girlfriend I was wondering if Thomas was feeling any better, you see he

dropped his wallet on his way out of the hospital," My aunt gave Anna a

quizzical look of suspicion and then opened the door to allow her to come

in. Anna stepped inside the house, "You have a very nice home, ma'am"

Anna said coyly. My aunt gave a small snort of approval and proceeded

into the kitchen.

"Have a seat," she said sharply, "I will get us some drinks, and see if

Thomas is up," Upon hearing my name, my heart raced as I slyly slid back

into my room and hid underneath my covers, pretending to be asleep.

Although I couldn't see what was happening, I could hear the poison of

Anna attitude drip from her teeth as she started condescending conversation through the air vent.

"So… *you* must be Thomas's new girlfriend," she said coolly. Lesli glanced up from the magazine she was reading.

"What…?" she asked innocently, "Who said anything about that, I hardly know him" Anna bull snorted and gave a flick of her hair, "besides we're going to be related soon, so it would be kind of weird,"

"Good, because he's my man, and I will do whatever it takes to keep him that way," she whispered nastily, "not every day you meet a class-A sucker, am I right?" Lesli cleared her throat, and continued reading her magazine.

"Hey, I am talking to you!" she said giving Lesli a violent push. Thankfully Lesli had her wheels locked in place.

"I heard you," she said calmly, "I just choose not to respond,"

"Well you're responding now, aren't you?" Anna retorted.

"Yes, but that's because your being rude, and I don't want to be like someone like you, "

"What is *that* supposed to mean?"

"You're smart, you can figure it out. Not *everyone* has to spell it out for you,"

"You're a real piece of work, you know that?" Anna snorted.

"You don't like it, and then you can leave. No one said you *had* to come in, you did that on your own,"

"You *are* a real piece of work," Anna fumed.

"No need to sound like a broken record," Lesli said simply, flipping through the pages.

Anna got up from the chair and circled around Lesli with a disdainful glare as she got down real close and whispered in her ear. "You really want to push me over the edge, because you are *this* close from me completely losing it," She said flicking open her switchblade threateningly, running the smooth, sharp blade against Lesli's pale skin. All the while, Aunt Flora was observing quietly, waiting to see what happens.

"Do your worst," Lesli said softly, "You won't like the outcome,"

I sat quietly listening to Anna's jealousy as her tone brought a sense of hostility to the room.

"Lesli…" I whispered softly

"Why don't you go back to the sea where you belong, freak," what happened next was unbelievable: Anna angrily opened the patio door and pushed Lesli down the hill as she began pushing her down the steep incline as I watched in horror as Lesli headed straight for the pond. Lesli attempted to put on her breaks, but the velocity of the speed was so immense that had she stopped, the force of ejection would be the same as if she was thrown from the car. The hill the house stood on was dangerous.

Anna wiped her hands together walking away from Lesli who tried to keep her head above the freezing pond water. I raced down the steps and confronted Anna who grabbed my arm and was going to drag me into the house. I couldn't ignore Lesli's cry for help, because she couldn't swim that well.

"What the hell is going on!" I screamed at Anna as I pushed her away and ran to help Lesli diving head first into the pond, fully clothed. Her blond hair was caked with duckweed as I brought her to the surface. She climbed on to the dock and sputtered out pond water. I dove in again and tried to retrieve her wheelchair. As I pulled on it, I knew that I wasn't going to be able to move it, so I left it and sprung myself onto the dock

"Anna, you get out of here right NOW!" I screamed.

"I am not going anywhere," Anna retorted in defiance. I stroked Lesli's hair pulling a piece of seaweed out of her hair, as disgusting as it felt. Anna sprang to pull me off of her, but seemed to be constricted by something, I turned my head, I saw Anna handcuffed together.

"Oh, yes you are. You are coming with me, you just messed with the wrong family," Anna looked at my aunt and then at me with an evil glare. "I will kill you!"

"Premeditated homicide? That will land you 60 years in prison," my aunt pulled her away from Lesli and myself and put her into the squad car

"I will be back," Aunt Flora called, "I got to book her, maybe a couple weeks in jail will keep her occupied," I nodded towards the car that pulled out of the driveway and flipped on her flashing lights, the resonating siren echoed through the neighborhood It felt good justice was beings served, even if it was to my soon-to-be-ex.

I found it kind of hard to believe that Anna would blow up on Lesli like that; her behavior is unlike have ever seen before. I carried Lesli into house and set her on the couch; she shivered a bit as her pale cheeks turned a rosy red her and her lips quivered in a blue tone. I went into the spare bedroom and pulled a wool blanket off the bedspread and wrapped it around her shoulders and got up to leave the room, but she tugged on my hand wanting me to keep her company. I looked at her and whistled for Max who came bounding into the living room and leaped on to the couch, placing his large head on to Lesli's lap. She sighed sadly and stroked Max, who began licking her chin. She giggled and snuggled with the husky. I made my exit out the patio door and towards the pond, and peered into the water, where the wheelchair was laying lazily on its side. Fish were already pecking at it curiously. I took off my shirt, and eased my way into the frigid water my body gave off an eerie shiver diving into the cold abyss. I swam down to the bottom of the pond kicking my feet as I circled the wheelchair, the cold water began to numb my muscles as I examined it with blurry vacant eyes. The water stung my eyes as hues of green swirled around me. I kicked my feet up to the surface and took a breath of air, before diving back into the depths of the pond. It was only a few moments time before I came back up for air, and swept my bangs out of my eyes, spitting out water. I caught the gaze of a man who was watching me with interest. I looked up at him, casting my gaze from his tan hard leather boots, to his military uniform. I blinked as he held out a hand to help me out of the water. I shook my head and declined it. He waited a few moments time for me to come up for air. He offered it to me again, I took his hand as he draped his jacket around my shoulders.

"A bit nippy for swimming," he said gruffly as he led me into the house. I didn't say a word. "You alright?" he asked softly. I whipped my hair out of my eyes, combing them with my fingers.

"Yeah, I am fine," I muttered softly. I handed him the jacket and went

upstairs to my room to put on a heavier sweater. I came downstairs and

glanced at the countertop where a set of keys was lying. A note read under

the keys:

Thomas, I am going to be late tonight. I am paying for the hospital visit

then I am going to the police station with Flora to file a restraining order.

Gene will be home shortly, will you pick up a cake for him? Mom.

I looked at Gene who was sitting patiently on the couch, video chatting

with his buddies on his iPad; by the sounds of the running water, I could

tell Lesli had made her way to the shower, I couldn't help but felt sorry for

the poor girl. The life she lived must have been hard I passed Gene who

hadn't noticed me, as I slipped out of the door silently. I looked down at

the ground fumbling with the keys to find the right one. I cast my gaze at

the parked car that remained dormant. When I looked up and my jaw

dropped as I gasped with excitement. "No way!" I gasped as I ran my

hand over the shimmering hull of the navy blue Ford Mustang. This

seemed to be true! Excitedly I entered the vehicle and turned on the car.

The riveting hum was like music as I checked over my shoulder and pulled into the street, accelerating on the gas—the quiet that to loomed

over the small town was instantly shattered.

<u>Chapter 3</u>

Thoughts inside my head transpired into a dull and vacant realm.

Nothing really seemed to perk my interest, as my tires sped around tight

corners. I honestly had no idea where I was going; no one had told me

how to get to town, and judging by my luck I was sure to get lost. I

stopped at a four-way intersection and sped my way across the street once

I saw it was clear. I kept glancing around searching for any means of

familiar routes, but it was all foreign to me. I sighed to myself in

frustration and looked around, when I noticed that the Mustang had an

onboard GPS system. I switched it on and typed in the nearest store once I

stopped safely at a stop sign.   I rolled down my window and let my arm

hang as I controlled the steering with my right hand. As I rounded another

corner, the eerie silence that haunted my thoughts was now replaced by an

unnerving howl that sounded painfully close. I pulled off to the side and

turned off my car as I listened to the howl. It was the most magnificent,

yet ominous thing I have ever heard. Wisconsin was only known for their

cows, cheese, and beer, so I never heard anything as majestically beautiful

as this wail. Sitting the driver's seat, a sharp shiver went down my spine.

Something inside of me felt misplaced, like the wolf wasn't howling out of loneliness, but out of pain, and despair. I got out of my car to investigate. Not far from where I entered, could I hear whining coming from a large black wolf that was caught in a bear trap. My heart leapt to my throat as I could feel my blood run cold. Golden eyes pierced my soul. I slowly made my way towards the animal. Every step I took, I could feel her pain, as she yelped, trying to release herself from the bear trap; every time she moved her paw, the trap dug deeper into her flesh and bone. My heart raced with anxiety as I was now only a few feet from this majestic hunter. She was scared…so was I. I knew she could sense it, and as a result, she bore her teeth menacingly. I took a deep breath and got down on my knees to examine the wound: the claw dug deep with a rusted embrace.

She tried to move her paw away from me, and yelped. I gulped and gave a soft smile, slowly working my hands toward her. At one point, she snapped her jaws at me, as sharp canines nicked the surface of my hand: the feeling was smooth, but razor sharp, never had I been so close to a wild animal before. The wolf whined and bit at her leg.

"Easy girl," I coaxed softly, "you're going to be fine; I will get you out of there."

I looked around for a piece of loose clothing to use as a bandage. I

34

noticed that I had a small rip in my right arm of the shirt. I dug my finger

into the hole to make it bigger, as I ripped off the clothing from the seam.

The wolf looked at me with her glinted golden eyes as she tilted her head

curiously. I reached my hand towards her paw, and lowered he nose to my

hand and sniffed; the wet, warm air that came from her nostrils tickled my

knuckle as she licked my hand softly. She whined once, but made no

sudden movements when I pried open the bear trap, blood gushed from

the open wound. Once her leg was free, I quickly applied the tourniquet as

she barked happily. Her tail wagged wildly as she pushed me down with

her paw, rubbing her face on me she licked my face rapidly with

appreciation. Upon applying pressure to her wounded paw, she yelped and

stumbled backwards looking at me with a tilted head. I got up to brush the

dirt off my pants. She barked once and nudging my hand with her nose I

pulled it away. She tilted her head and whined as if to ask *what did I do?* I

began to walk away and she began to follow me. The leaves crunch under

her paw, and I turned around and put a hand up.

"No, you have to *stay*," I said. The wolf whined and tucked her tail

between her legs as she limped into the forest. I watched her leave and

sighed to myself, walking back to the car. I opened up the door and sat in

the driver's seat and let myself calm down. My heart was still beating wickedly fast. The adrenalin that coursed through my veins made me feel light headed. I leaned my head back on the head rest and blacked out from too much excitement.

My thoughts were vague and distorted as my mind led me to believe I was in a world of disillusions. I wasn't sure what was happening, but I felt like I had been here before. I stood behind a tree as watched a man sit comfortably in a recliner in front of television set. The cabin windows flickered with a translucent golden hue. Inside the window, I could clearly see that light oak wooden flooring complimented the rustic interior design, however something didn't seem right: the room was covered in pelts— wolf pelts. Taxidermy wolf status stood near the fire place, as wolf heads hung delicately above, and wolf tails hung on both sides of the mantle. I inched closer to get a better look at the luminescent window, but was quickly taken off guard by the sound of a honking horn. I gasped when I saw the man pierce beady red eyes directly at me. I turned around and ducked out of the way only to see a shell of my Mustang driving through the forest, ushering me to get out of the way with flashing lights and a blaring horn. I stood and watched in horror as the car crashed its body into the side of the house, sending the man into visceral rage. I could see the man in the recliner get up to throw things, and set the house on fire, it was as intense as I ran for my life. The Mustang horn echo seemed to follow

me. No matter where I ran, it was tracking me down. My dream ended

from the pain of my neck cramping up from sleeping on my shoulder. I

groaned painfully and softly, massaged my aching neck. Turning on the

car, my heart skipped a beat when I realized that it was nearly six o'clock;

I left the house at two. I have been gone for *four* hours. I turned the

ignition on and started on my way. My mind was numb as I drove down

the silent strip of eroded concrete. Patches of thick tar were drizzled lazily

amongst the patches of hazardous pot holes as if the road workers were

too lazy to finish the job. I rolled to a stop sign, and craned my neck to the

left wincing in pain as I checked for any oncoming vehicles. After a brief

moment, I commenced to follow minivan that had the silhouette of two

fighting children in the back. The taillights faded into a blur as I followed

her to the next stoplight. Switching on to my right turn signal, I entered

the vicinity of a small strip mall I parked my car near the door and headed

into the grocery store. Walking down the aisle lazily, I looked at the cakes

with a vacant stare, quite honestly, I had forgotten what the cake was for,

regardless I picked up an extravagant double chocolate cake with brownie

bites embedded into the crust. Luckily it was on special, so I didn't pay as

much. I placed my merchandise at the counter and handed the clerk the money, where she in turn gave me my change and receipt.

I could not think of anything else except the wild wolf encounter I had. Gently I brushed my left hand over the top of my right. I could still feel the cold nose of the black wolf as the tongue flicked gently over my skin in gratitude. I smiled and placed the food in the backseat of the car. Closing the door, I turned on the ignition and proceeded home without the GPS. I needed time to think, more importantly I needed answers to why and how my dreams were becoming related.

Chapter 4

Ambivalent thoughts coerced my body to shut down both mentally
and emotionally. I wasn't at all sure what was happening, but for some
reason, I felt numb. My mind grew blank from all other functions except
for driving, and the memories that haunted me. The road turned into a blur
as I sped down the silent road. My thoughts were constantly beating
themselves against the silent prison which my brain had encased them. I
glanced at my speedometer as I passed a police car. The flashing lights
and the resonating siren broke me out of my fixated trance as I glanced in
my rear view mirror. My heart raced as I realized I had broken the law.
The lights in my rear view mirror continued to echo throughout my car as
I became conflicted as opposed to what to do. Normally people would pull
over, and accept the ticket and go on with their lives, but I wasn't going to
let that happen. It was bad enough that I had a police record since I was
eight, how would my revoked freedom fix any other problems I had with
the law? So I did the thing that most people only see on television or
movies—I floored it. The Mustangs' engine revved as I sped down the
busy highway, bursting through full speed through red lights. People
honked their horns and slammed on their brakes to flip off the rogue

driver that zipped past them trying to escape the pursuer. I glanced in my rearview mirror as I passed the police station, and noticed that two more police cars came out to pursue the Mustang. Wailing sirens riveted the attention of other drivers with their echoing cry throughout the city as I weaved through cars and ignored stop signs. The police officers followed my car for what seemed a good half hour before I turned on to eroded road that was soon shrouded in the presence of thick tree's that gave of an eerie, apprehensive atmosphere. In my last failed attempts to ditch the police, I pulled over, and made a break for it into the depths of the wooded abyss. I ran as far as I could while occasionally glancing over my shoulder. Beams of light from the police officers flash light bounced off the thick vegetation, as their feet trampled the earth. Distinct yelling to spread out and corner was ordered. I ran through the forest not really sure how far I was going to go, before my legs would give up on me. I could feel the presence of something lurking in the woods as I kept running. My thoughts of how to escape these police officers were suddenly shattered when I felt myself hit the ground at full force, while my hands were forcibly tied behind my back in cold metal handcuffs.

"Thought you could get away from us, huh kid? You gave us one hell of a fight," the police officer retorted as I laid there on the cold dirt. I knew, it wasn't going to end well, but I thought I might as well give it a shot. The police officer pulled me up by the hair as I yelped in pain. As my cry for help echoed through the forest, the sound of low chuffing could be heard as the full moon illuminated the clearing of the forest. Twigs snapped and vegetation rustled as the police officers looked around, feeling the presence of an ominous force lurk through the tree lines. The chuffing turned into a snarl as golden eyes pierced the blackness of the night. I gulped as the police officer tightened his grip on me, causing me to let out another yelp of pain. The chuffing changed into snarling ferocity as a lone black wolf stepped out of the forest to confront the officers. Teeth bore sharp as he size rendered immense. My eyes shifted up to the wolf as the officer pushed me to the ground and pulled out his gun.

"No!" I screamed, as I kicked my leg from underneath him, causing him to fall, setting off his gun. The bullet whizzed through the wolf's ear, leaving a small hole in the cartilage, much like an earring would leave. The wolf snarled as its hackles raised, lunging at the police officer. Each officer fired their gun trying to stop the monster, while all I could do was remain helpless. The wolf was agile, even for its size. The lupine swatted her large paw at one officer, sending him into a tree splicing him in half, while he bit the leg of another, and finally snapped the neck of the one I had kicked down.

The officers watched in horror as they retreated out of the forest, while other wolves tackled them to the ground, gnawing and slashing them in feral defiance. I couldn't see what had happened to the officers, due to the mud that stung my eyes. However, I could hear them scream and beg for mercy. Before the forest was rendered into an eerie silence. The howling of the wolves in the distance indicated that the hunt was over, and that a feast had been brought upon them. I sat up in the dirt as the wolf looked at me and panted. I looked at her paw which still had its bandage wrapped around tightly. The wolf nudged me softly with her large nose, as she placed her canines around my handcuffs and snapped her jaws together as the metal broke in two. It nudged me again whining as I pet its muzzle softly, as a soft tongue flicking against my hand in reassurance as they curled her thick coat around me protectively just as I have done for them; a beautiful bond and I couldn't help let out a contented sigh of admiration. The feeling happiness and warmth and thus sleep was an impeccable outcome.

I awoke early and noticed I was alone. I sat up in slowly and wondered if what I had seen the night before was another dream. The sun was just beginning to peak through the horizon as I stepped carefully over the mutilated bodies of the fallen officers. I grunted with disgust, "definitely not a dream," I couldn't help but feel guilty over the loss. I mean, these men had *families* and I let them suffer a horrible fate because I   wanted to escape the law. I sighed to myself, as I walked through the forest, feeling an ominous presence lurk behind me. I turned around quickly, but only heard the sounds birds chirping and rabbits running, I turned back around and gasped as I nearly stumbled over someone in a wheelchair who had a gun in his hand.

"Just *what* do you think you're doing, here boy?" The man asked.

"I got lost," I mumbled, eyeing the gun nervously.

"No one *just* gets lost in here, boy, either you know the place or you don't. If you do, then you're a visitor, if you don't then you're a trespasser," I glanced at the man's wheelchair for a brief moment before he gave a disdainful glare through thick aviator glasses.

"Eyes on me, boy," he scolded coldly. I looked at him with a small bit of an aggravated expression. "You got some nerve coming around these parts, its best if you leave, before those wolves get to you,"

"So you've seen them," I asked, quickly changing the subject.

"Yeah, I have, but I wouldn't advise you to go looking for them, they're a wild bunch. Why they killed two armed officers last night. Scary as hell,"

he muttered. "But enough chit-chat, get out of here, before I decide to do a

little target practice on your puny little head," I snorted and walked past

him, "look who is being called puny." I muttered silently.

"Oh, and kid, don't let me catch you around here, no more. These are

dangerous territories," he snorted and wheeled away. I couldn't figure out

what the man was talking about. *Dangerous territories, what did he*

mean? Surly he wasn't talking about the wolves....they were protecting

me, weren't they? I sighed to myself and glanced around the road, noticing

the car was surrounding by inoperable cop cars.

"*Great!*" I muttered to myself. I passed by the cars, and noticed that one

of them still had the keys in the ignition. I entered the vehicle, and moved

it out of the path of my car. Looking through the car, I noticed my VIN on

the computer screen my police records showed warrants for my arrest. I

noticed a corner sticking out of the glove compartment. I opened the glove

compartment and found a strange yet beautiful picture, but gasped to my

horror. The picture revealed two young couples on a beach in Florida. One

of the couples was my dad and a mysterious woman who wasn't my

mother. Flipping over the photo was an inscription *with love your mistress, Danica.* My heart sank when I realized that my father was one of the officers that were trying to protect me, and he was now dead.

I stumbled hazily through the front door of my aunt's house and crashed on the couch. It had only been a couple minutes before I was awoken by thumping footsteps coming down the stairs. I didn't know what was happening, but the next thing I knew I was up against the wall with a violent glare fixating on my dilated pupils.

"The hell have you been?" the gruff voice demanded. I couldn't speak from the shock and confusion. I felt my back hit the wall once more as I heard another set of steps race down wooden stairs.

"Gene, stop!" My aunt cried in a frantic as she tried to pull the deranged military officer off of me.

"Stay out of this, Flora!" he said coldly. Aunt Flora did her best to pull him off of me once again, but this only made him angrier causing him to instinctually backhand his fiancé, causing her to fall to the ground with a bruised eye and bloody lip.

"No, Gene, I will not. That is my nephew, and this is America, not Russia, now let him go, unless you want to spend time in a cell for assaulting a police officer," she threatened. Gene's shoulders loosened as he dropped me to the floor. I slumped against the wall with pain searing through my skull. She glared at Gene for a moment before draping an arm around me helping me up the stairs to my bedroom. She sighed softly as she laid me on my bed as she went down stairs for a few minutes, bringing me water and Aspirin. She shook her head softly, as she exited my room, closing the door only a crack. I felt nauseous. The room felt like it was spinning and everything felt like it was on a slant. I took the medicine and laid my head on the soft pillow covering my face with another pillow. The cold side of the pillow felt good against my face as I closed my eyes. I still felt the room was spinning, but managed to ignore it as I fell asleep.

<u>Chapter 5</u>

Rap-tap-tap the sound of elongated fingers on the tall oak tree by my window taunted my slumber. The wind blew fiercely as rain pounded against the roof of the house. Kind thoughts ran in fright as frightening images danced in my subconscious mind. Hypnotic jerks kept me from gaining pleasant sleep, and when I did finally sleep it was only for a short while before panic erupted in me, fear that if I fell asleep, I would be late for something important. Nothing but vivid images of the police officers corpses laying in a mangled mess coerced me into an insomniac state. As I sat in bed, I rubbed my eyes and blinked a few times allowing my eyes adjust to the darkness. I planted my feet on the cool floor, opening my door just a smidge, I squeezed through and headed down the stairwell with my hand gripping tightly to the banister. As I cast my eyes around the dim-lit room. Thunder crashed in the horizon and lighting flashed filling the room with light. In a brief moment of that flash there was a dark shadow standing outside the patio door. Squinting my eyes, I tried to make out the figure, the shape was stout and disfigured, I blinked, and the shadow melded into the background of the night. I remained silent for a long time. Gene was fast asleep on the couch snoring silently; Aunt Flora must have kicked him out of the bedroom for the stunt he pulled. I leaned over the banister and looked out the window, watching the storm. The picture I obtained from the police car hung loosely in my hand as I traced my finger over my father's face. I sighed as I looked at him smiling with his arm around his mistress. I heard so many stories of this heartless witch: according to Aunt Flora, rumor has it that Danica was a mysterious woman who was running from political prosecution. After she smuggled herself across the border, she was a woman of many false aliases to avoid being found. She often forged identification cards, just to surpass the risk of being deported. She met my father while serving a warrant for her arrest. He was succumbed by lust from Danica as she explained she had nowhere to go and was with child. Feeling guilty, Mr. Bravier took her in under protective custody and forged a green card for her to stay, but luck was about to change when my mother found out about the affair, and ordered a divorce. When asked to appear in court with his mistress, one of the federal agents recognized Danica and was arrested. When she tried to explain that she was pregnant, no one seemed to buy it, until she lifted up her shirt to show that she was in fact with child—the court ruled that she be placed under house arrest until she delivered the baby. After the child was born, Danica was deported back to Russia with child, where she was killed on arrival. Not sure what to do with the child, the Russians left it in a basket, swaddled in warm clothes, placing it in the forest where they prayed that its life would end soon, and be out of its misery. It just so happened that an hour after dropping off the baby, a local Native tribe found the baby and took it in as their own naming it: "Frozen Lost Cub." Many answers remained unsolved as opposed to whether the legend was true or not, but that would explain why Brandon would often yell in another language when he got mad, and when my mother asked him where he picked it up, he would always reply: "Chief Shinaak."

I stood there on the landing with lightning illuminating my path way back up the steps. I crawled back in bed and sighed as thunder continued to rumble; rain tapping rhythmically against the shingled roof. I finally managed to fall asleep, for what seemed to be a few hours but was awoken by a cold draft wafting through the room. I opened my eyes slowly and looked around. The shutters flailed in wind as I made my way to close the window. The cold tiles was like ice against my bare feet as a pool of rainwater formed from the drenched storm window. I began to close the window, but stopped when I saw a dark shadow moving along the edge of the woods. Looking into the darkness, I slowly scaled out of my shimmed down the trellis, trudging my way through to the backyard. The damp grass sloshed under my feet as I headed towards the forest clearing. I stopped short a few feet of the forest looking around. I wasn't sure what I was looking at, but deep golden eyes pierced through the thickets. I stepped forward as the eyes watched my movement. I stepped towards the forest slowly, making slow, but cautious movements. The eyes retreated into the forest as a firm hand grasped on to my shoulder. Turning around I was surprised to see my Aunt Flora standing there in her pink night gown, gazing at me with concern. I looked at for a moment before turning my head to the forest, scanning my eyes to see if I could catch a glimpse of those yellow orbs.

"Thomas?" she asked softly. My only response was a slow murmur of incoherent mumbling She spoke my name again, and I turned to walk past her towards the house. As I made my way to the door, a violent shiver went down my spine as I felt cold eyes watch my every move. I softly sighed to myself and shook the rain out of my eyes before entering the house.

Morning was hazy from last night's storm. I sat at the breakfast nook and stirred my coffee slowly, watching the brown liquid with disinterest. Flora was the first to come down, and greet me.

"Morning," she said pouring herself a cup. I looked up at her and smiled a little bit before going back to stirring my cup groggily. She sat down in front of me and put a hand on wrist and rubbed it soothingly. Her soft, cold hand seemed to awaken my senses that made me stop stirring.

"I am worried about you," she said softly.

"Why?" I mumbled.

"You've been acting strangely," she replied. I scoffed and looked at her and took a sip of my coffee. Strong, Smooth brew slid down my throat as I let out a soft contented sigh. I thought about commenting on her, but decided against it. I took another sip of coffee before responding to her.

"I will be fine," I lied. She let out a sigh of concern and frustration.

"I don't think you are," her statements made me cringe as I pounded my fist on the table causing the coffee to jump out of its ceramic encasement.

"How could you *possibly* know?" I demanded, "You know *nothing* about me!" I scolded. Her eyes looked hurt as she tried to touch my hand again in a soothing manner. I quickly pulled it away and stood up heading towards the door.

"Thomas..." she began. I turned and looked at her, but said nothing. I shook my head and turned the knob leaving the house in a brisk haste. The atmosphere drizzled lightly as I walked down the long narrow driveway, my hands dug into my pockets and my eyes fixated on the road.

I stopped for a moment only to realize where I was. Trees loomed high above the skyline; the thick haze shrouded the base of the tree as I walked to a broken sign hanging on a branch.

Danger! Timber Falls has swift currents and deadly undertows. Keep off cliffs.

I looked up at the trees and scanned the intriguing structure: low branches arched around the entry of the forest, where light became obsolete by the pitch black abyss of the shady forest. What really struck me as odd were tire tracks that lead into the forest, the tire tracks cut a medium width groove into the dirt that looked like ATV tracks. Following the tracks I was lead deep into uncharted terrain as the thickness of the forest closed in on me. Taking careful steps into the mysterious domain, I couldn't help but overhear boisterous shouting as engines revved. I ducked behind a large boulder and watched as men in thick burly beards and large plaid shirts haul wooden crates on to a truck. The crates had large air holes in the sides. Men yelled orders as tires continued to squeal with an awful grinding noise; it seemed that one of the trucks was stuck in the mud. Tilting my head, I looked from behind the boulder trying my best to keep hidden, but something didn't feel right. I felt the barrel of a gun against the side of my temple as a gruff hand places a hand on my throat.

"Well, Well, Well. Looks like we have ourselves a visitor," the voice said.

I didn't bother looking around as I slowly stood up, but the gruff hand

pushed me back to the ground with brute force.

"No one said you could move," he said darkly. My throat grew dry as I

felt dark eyes glare at me.

"I warned you once boy, about wandering around these dangerous parts.

You walked into the wrong territory, now you will pay the price" He

snarled briskly.

"Shall I shoot him here?" a voice asked. The voice hesitated then darkly

growled with a sinister grin. "No, he wants to meet my pet? We'll see how

friendly they are when they are fighting over his carcass," My heart

stopped briefly as my blood ran cold. The gruff hand lifted me up by the

shirt collar and pushed me towards torturing device. Two large wooden

poles were planted firmly in the ground. It looked like it was used for

hanging dead dear, to keep the bears from getting at it. On top of the

poles were chains hung loosely at the sides. The gruff man hoisted me up

to the pole and shackled my arms and legs to the contraption. I felt

helpless. I tried to pull my arms free, but the device held me tight. A long

distinct whistle came from the mouth of the man as wolves bounded from

open crates. Gruff snarling and deranged jaws snapped viscously as they were only inches from my legs, as if they were toying with me, trying to make me flinch. Fear enveloped me as I looked at the feral beasts. The man let out another whistle and nodded as he unleashed the animals which went straight for my throat. I closed my eyes tight waiting for the pain to come. Much to my surprise, I felt my feet fall to the ground. I opened up my eyes and looked around. A pack of wolves the size of a horse were standing guard over me. Their sharp canines bared as the she-wolf stood on top of a small hill looking down at her small army. Manny rolled up, and snarled, taking off his dark glasses to glare at the she-wolf, taking off his glasses revealing a deep scratch across his left orb as the infection has claimed his precious sight in that eye.

"You're a damned traitor," he snarled. The wolf raised her hackles and gave a low, threatening growl as she made her way down to the man. He snorted and rolled towards the wolf with an evil glare.

"I thought we had a deal: You bring me the boy and I won't cage you like the useless mutt that you are," he growled. The wolf padded towards him, until her muzzle was only inches away, rippling a threatening growl in front of his face, she snarled and then sneezed, spraying snot on him as she snorted in defiance. Manny growled and smacked her across the face. The she wolf snarled and grabbed Manny by the wrist, snapping it in half as she ripped him out of his wheel chair, throwing him against the tree.

A feral beast war of violence broke out as guns were fired and teeth clashed against fur and skin. Yelps of pain and snarls of anger could be heard from the distance as I ran deep into the woods. I felt a powerful force follow close beside me, as vicious growls followed my scent. Twigs and branches snapped as blurs of grey moved swiftly and effortless through the foliage.

My breath grew raspy as I pushed heavy leaves out of my path. Heavy panting could be heard as I continued to run. I wasn't sure how far from the camp I was, but I had to keep pressing forward. It wasn't until I reached the edge of the cliff when I stopped to catch my breath. I pressed my hands on my knees as my hair hung loosely over my eyes. I stopped and turned around, feeling cold, hungry eyes close in on me. I stood there frozen and cornered, waiting…

Chapter 6

A white flash of fur moved in for the kill. I could see the ferocity in their eyes as they constricted a hungry expression. I felt a sharp pain in my rib as teeth clenched down on my abdomen causing warm blood oozed out of the puncture wounds. I could feel something heavy ram its body into my stomach, pushing me off the edge of the cliff. The rush of a heavy waterfall masked my yelp of surprise as I headed straight into the lakebed below. Swirling oxygen bubbles escaped my mouth as frigid waters the heavy undertows claimed my semi-conscious body. I could still hear and see things, but not enough to make sense of what they were. I felt something grab my shirt collar, and pull me to shore with little to no effort. A thick blanket of temporary blindness clouded my vision as I remained in an altered state of shock—though something did seem to bring me back to reality: the warmth of breath and the tickling sensation of a soft tongue raking across my face. I blinked and scrunched my nose as I smelled an unfamiliar musk.

Opening one eye, I slowly began to come to consciousness. It wasn't until I was fully alert when I realized what had happened as I glanced up at the free falling water that seemed to pour out of a large cavern that gave the illusion that the rock formation of a wolf's head was "drooling". I was once again rescued by a wild wolf. I looked around and I noticed a massive white paw was just inches away from my foot, I smiled gratefully at the extremely large lupine. The size was approximately the size of a horse, it looked around, smelling the air, and padded to the water's edge for a drink. It's large tail swaying like a pendulum against its thick muscular hindquarters. Lapping the water, it quickly lifted a head and stared at me before taking another drink. I winced a few times as I positioned myself. The wolf perked its ears and whined as I lifted my shirt to look at the inflicting puncture wounds. Fresh blood flowed, as the wolf sniffed the air again, setting off a long and mournful howl.

Large black figures appeared at the top of the cliff and looked down at us before heading back into the forest. The large white wolf snorted and turned its head towards me before padding back to my location and lowering its head to rub against my chest. It gave a small growl of pleasure as it continued to rub with affection. I flexed my fingers and offered my hand to the lupine, the wolf commenced to lick my fingers as it pressed its head into them. I smiled and rubbed its wet coat. It wasn't long before I turned my head and sneezed. The wolf perked her ears and tilted its head watching me with curious golden eyes. I sneezed again and it stood up towering over me. A large shadow engulfed my pale skin as it gently knelt down on its legs and whined, pawing at my leg. I sneezed again any it let out a small, but deep bark. I looked at the large wolf and it whined, lowering its head close to my cheek and giving it a lick of concern before resting its head on my lap. The thick fur covered my legs like a large blanket. I smiled at the wolf, as I looked to the sky just as gray clouds shrouded the sun as a foggy haze drifted into view.

"Let's get out of here," I murmured. The wolf stood up and barked wagging its tail briskly giving me a lick on the cheek. It put its mouth around my arm and gently pulled me to my feet. I patted its side and it looked back at me with ears perked, waiting and whining. I tilted my head and it lifted its hind leg to scratch her ear before setting it down. I stood there confused for a moment before I realized what she was implying. The wolf sat on her haunches and I walked behind her, feeling the tail sway with excitement. I gently stepped on her back leg. She lifted her hind leg up to help me up for a better mount. Once situated, I moved closer to the front of her spine and sat there for a moment. It was rather different feeling being on the back of a wolf; her body was slender and muscular, as riveting sensation it was! Her thick fur buried my thighs as my feet hung loosely behind her front legs. She shook her large white pelt and panted with excitement as I looked around. She sniffed the ground before

stealthily heading into the forest. I sat perfectly still upon the back if the

wolf, only moving to pet her soft pelt. Her soft panting echoed through the

soft underbrush as she carefully stepped over fallen logs and forest debris,

slinking her frame through the brush, she crouched into a hunting pose, as

her shoulder blades raised through her pelt. She stopped and sniffed the

air, twitching her ears and turned around. I could feel her hackles rise

slightly as she gave a low warning snarl. I couldn't see what was going on,

but I could sense that we wandered on to foreign territory. She walked

over to a large tree and stopped. I dismounted and climbed a tree for a

better view, watching with interest. Her deep white pelt stood on end as I

watched a pack of timber wolves creep out of the shadows confronting her

in a haughty manner.

Golden eyes watched their movements with narrow slits, as they began

taunt her, snapping their   jaws together. She looked at the tree to see if I

was okay, and then back at the wolves who were circling her. A warm

breath went down my neck as I felt wet rubber touch my skin. I dared not

draw attention, but it seems the wolves were causing a riot, snapping their

jaws at her feet. She swatted at one, but another took a bite out of her leg.

A long warm tongue went down my shirt as I felt the warm breath pant steadily against my flesh. I turned around slightly, only to realize that my face was inches away from another large wolf. It licked its jowls and then gave me a slurp on the face. I shrieked in surprise as I backed away from the large beast. The gray wolf tilted its head and moved its head forward to sniff me. It whined as I backed away from it. The white wolf turned its head towards me, and gave a large snarl as it pulled me out of the tree by the shirt collar. She threw her head back and I slid down her furry neck and on to her back. Rubbing my neck, I felt the thick saliva cling to my fingers. I gave a disgusted scoff, and wiped the slime on my pants. The large gray wolf sat on its haunches and raised a paw towards the female wolf I was mounted on. She backed away slowly and the timber wolves hoisted their rears on the air in a playful bow position. I quickly caught on to what was happening: the large gray wolf was the alpha and the smaller wolves were the betas. They were playing with us.

The white wolf gave a slight nod, and barked. The gray wolf and his pack swayed their tails with delight. Sensing no greater harm, I dismounted and greeted the timbers with a smile on my face, the white wolf nodded and nuzzled my cheek with affection...I finally understood: This was her family.

<u>Chapter 7</u>

A jolt of pain traveled through my body as an uneasy gurgling forced me into an upright position against the soft fur of the wolf. I did my best to ignore the pain as I lay on my side, feeling the warmth of the fur and the steady breathing raise and lower to the beating heart. A funky musk entered my nostrils as I lay perfectly still. My stomach churned as a painful bolt shot through my body and into my bladder. I sat up clenching my stomach almost feeling embarrassed to leave. Slowly sitting up, I looked around: the timbers slept soundly huddled against their father, who lay on his side, cold cavern floor touching his right side of his face. I looked towards the exit, where the moon shone brightly. Carefully I made my way towards the door looking over my shoulder to see the white wolf once more. Her face was tucked in her tail, and she lay in a large ball. Her ears twitched listening to the sounds around her.

I followed a silent path through the woods to find the perfect spot that had both privacy and lighting. As I sat there against the tree, a slight shiver went down my spine; I could feel a set of eyes watching me, but from which direction I could not tell. *Was the she wolf following me, making sure I was okay?* I hadn't the slightest idea. I scrounged around for a pile

of leaves and quickly cleaned myself up before heading to the stream.

That same uneasy feeling wouldn't quit haunting me. The nervous shiver

kept flowing down my spine. I knelt down on the river bank and washed

off my hands, occasionally listening for any sign of danger.

I headed back to camp, in the direction I thought I came. A feeling of

dread washed over me as I looked at the trees—every last one looked

exactly the same. The feeling if being watched didn't help my paranoia

either. My mind played tricks as images danced to the tune of the

forbidden songs of night. I looked around frantically and clenched my fists

in anger.

"Come on out you coward!" I demanded. Nothing moved except for

the occasional sound of rustling branches that swayed in the calm breeze. I

took a step back and bumped into something solid, and thick with coarse

hair. A slop of pungent water landed on my shoulder as I felt heavy

breathing blow through my hair. I spun around and gasped, stumbling

backwards landing on the ground, I scrounged around and picked up a

large stick. There, standing before me was a great demon of the night.

Shrouded in black, with twelve inch fangs bared and breathe reeking of

decaying corpses. Paws stood at attention as claws gripped the earth, creating trench-like grooves in the hard soil. Eyes glinted and bewildered with a deviled glare. Dried blood was caked to the beasts muzzle as a smooth tongue ran over its fangs, savoring the blood that remained.

A lone cloud moved out of the range of the moons glistening rays to reveal man who sat proudly with a gun clenched firmly in his hand.

"Well, well," the man sneered, "look who came crawling back, and for what, to see my magnificent beasts. You don't really think that twig of yours is going to protect you against nine hundred pounds of muscle?" he snorted as he shifted his weight.

"Let me ask you something: if by chance you *do* manage to make it out alive, who's going to believe you? These are restricted grounds, any sort of knowledge that you've been here, and you can find yourself in a heap of trouble, and God knows you don't need a criminal record, now do you Thomas?" he taunted, "I will tell you what: I will go easy on you since you're a first offender, I will shoot you first, then let Ember here take care of the rest."

My heart raced with adrenaline as I kept the stick firmly on my hand. I glared at the man who loaded bullets into his gun, and cocked it with the ammunition.

"Don't worry about them looking for you; I highly doubt anyone will find your body." he chuckled and aimed at me before firing. The shot went off, and I flinched, I didn't feel any pain. I blinked and looked around and saw that the man was thrown off his mount by an unseen force. His gun was knocked out of his hands and I made a dash for it. The black beast was faster than me, and blocked my path from escaping. Hackles raised as a sinister snarl erupted from her throat. It pawed the ground and flicked its tongue through its teeth revealing a pink gum line, saliva dripping from her wicked fangs. I circled the beast half way before darting in the other direction. Yelps of pain and desperation echoed in the night from the man.

"Ember, help me!" he pleaded, "forget the boy, save me first." The black wolf shook her head glancing at the human who was being constrained by the timber wolves. Each wolf clenched down on the man's arms and while they put their full weight of 150 pounds on each arm. Ember looked back at me, deep red eyes catching my glare. Raising my weapon and charged at her, pointing the sharp end of the javelin towards her; she snarled and bounded towards me with vicious speed, dirt flying through the air as a jolt of black fur blended into the background, if it wasn't for her glowing eyes, I wouldn't have stood a chance against this monster. I immediately I ducked and rolled to avoid her teeth, claws were only inches away from my face. The wolf skidded to a halt, and snorted before lunging again, this time with accurate precision. I heard teeth

clench as sharp enamel braised my ear, the man jeered but was quickly

replaced by a yelp of pain as the timber dug their teeth into his arms. The

wolf stopped and snorted showing her wicked fangs before letting out a

growl of determination. I clenched the stick tighter and aiming the sharp

end for her throat, just a pole-vaulter aimed for their goal. The beast

dodged and swatted me to the ground, sharp claws raking against my side,

leaving twelve-inch grooves across my chest. I stood up breathing hard

and feeling faint from battle and from my newly obtained wound. I

stumbled towards her wearily with determination as the man yelled with

sheer devilish delight, which was once again silenced with a shriek of

pain. I charged at her, and the wolf charged back with open jaws, but

something pushed me out of the way—the white wolf.

The large female snarled and tackled the black demon to the ground.

Vicious snarls broke the tranquility of the night. I stumbled towards the

white wolf, but was pushed back down by a firm but gentle paw--the alpha

was protecting me from the ferocious dog fight. The fight raged on until

the break of dawn; as the sun peeped over the horizon, I witnessed the

conclusion of the horrific battle: the black wolf latched on to the scruff of

the white wolfs neck and twisted it. The pleading yelp echoed through the forest with a terrifying *crack!* the black wolf dropped the white wolfs

body—she was dead; blood erupted from the puncture wounds as the

demon laid down and began to roll all over the white wolf, crushing bone

and marking her scent over her kill. She then stood up and shook her pelt,

before walking back into the thick underbrush leaving Manny lay

unconscious, not bothering to take him with.

Chapter 8

The shrill of an ambulance was enough to put anyone's mood on

edge, thankfully, I wasn't the one that the EMTs were treating. I stood and

watched the commotion with glinted eyes. A man half the size of me was

being continuously shocked through resuscitation. Electrical currents

flowed through his body causing it to jerk violently, as the EMT

desperately did their best to revive him. Another jolt went through his

body causing to twitch. More sirens wailed through the night as a team of

police and fire fighters barricaded the entrance to the forest. I watched a

team of forensic scientists haul the remains of the white wolf and place

them into a sterile van. I winced silently as I shifted my weight and slunk

back into the abyss, turning my attention to watch the EMT close the

ambulance doors and drive off—sirens once again shattering the tranquil

night. I sighed to myself and looked at the large gray wolf. His ears folded

back against his head, his gaze lowered to the ground. Prolonged sorrow

as tears diluted his crisp golden eyes into a pale yellow. I could feel his

pain—it was the same way I felt when I lost my brother. He nudged a wet,

rubbery nose into my arm, until he nestled it under my armpit. I stroked his smooth, coarse hair as he whined gently. I looked at the timbers and they lowered their heads, clenching their tails under their stomachs; their actions almost too pitiful to bear. I pushed the wolf's nose out of my armpit and looked at him square in the eyes. A long, slender tongue swept across my face as the wolf sought comfort and empathy from me. I walked past him, and he padded behind slowly, giving off a small bark. I stopped and turned my head as I watched him lower his body to the ground. I walked to his side, and gently mounted his pelt, using his foreleg as boost. I glanced at the two timbers tat trailed behind somberly—suddenly stopping to let out a long and ominous howl. I gently clenched the wolf's scruff as he stood up. The two timbers trailed behind slowly, as if to be in a train of thought. My hand clenched tightly on to the coarse fur as I gritted my teeth-I wanted revenge, and I wanted it *now*.

I slept soundly on the back of the large canine; the breeze rustling through my hair and the swaying of its body made it seem like I was on a boat as waves rolled gently under the hull. Images of a pearly white goddess that took on the form of a white wolf challenge every aspect of reality: The pristine wolf ran through the forest with grace, and beauty. Her white coat reflected off rich leather mahogany. The tree lines were smooth and glossy as her thick pelt brushed effortlessly past them. The wolf skidded to a halt and stopped near a bank of a river where crystal water flowed freely. An owl perched on a nearby olive tree as the wolf turned around sensing my presence. Her eyes were clear and vivid—filled with emotion that indicated that she was wise and honorable. Her ears perked as she snapped her head in the other direction sensing something that was unforeseen: a silent howl of another wolf. She gave a small snort of disapproval as she glanced at me before bounding into the forest. I tried to follow her, but the trees began to close in on me, pushing me out of the sacred forest. The owl stared at me, and ruffled its feathers preening them before it flying off. I was shaken from my dream as I felt myself land on the ground. I groggily looked around in mild shock as I watched the flanks of the wolf disappear into the thick underbrush. I was back where I stared—Aunt Flora's house.

*****

The wedding layout was absolutely astounding: the vivid imagery was so serene that it looked like it would have been captured in a *National Geographic* magazine. I smiled and cast my gaze over the land: pearly white chairs were aligned perfectly next to each other, rows of fifteen on each side of a large aisle; the alter was decorated with custom made bamboo poles where an American Flag hung freely as a backdrop. I sighed contently as I watched the sun peek through rows of evergreens. A rough hand grasped my shoulder with a gentle, but firm grip. I looked at to my left and scaled my eyes to meet with Gene's.

"I may not always be in sync with your erratic behavior," he began, "but that doesn't mean I should be so strict. You're a kid, and kids got to learn from experience." I kept silent trying to figure out what he was talking about, "I know you've been going into the forest at night, and visiting the wolves...and I don't blame you, I did the exact same thing when I was a kid," I felt my heart lighten a little bit as a soft burden began to lift off my shoulders, "but I don't want you to go there without a companion—it's not safe. Especially with that black demon." My eyebrows shot up in surprise as I bit my lip before I found the courage to speak up, feeling a little ashamed.

"It killed a white wolf," I said.

"Damn," Gene snorted a sigh.

I cocked my head to the side at his reaction wondering what he meant.

"I always knew Athena had it in her, but never thought she was crazy enough to get herself killed," Gene released his grip from my shoulder and stood at attention. "Then again, she has been so sick lately... she was suffering from distemper. God rest her soul. I raised her from a pup when her parents were shot by hunters-but then things got ugly when Manny

found out about her," I looked at him with a quizzical expression.

"Manny?" I asked. Gene looked away and shook his head.

"That man is a lethal genius. He graduated from college when he was

in his late twenties with a degree in Biochemical Engineering. He found a

way to alter L-ornithine Hydrochloride...a growth hormone if you will—

make the amino acids in an animal's body grow in incredible sizes. When

the government found out about his practice, they confiscated his creation

and shut down his operation. He was livid; he stormed into the

government facility and demanded that his creation be returned to him at

once. When they refused, he took his creation by force and fled. He knew

he was a wanted criminal, and he would do whatever it to make sure that

his creation was safe," I looked down at my feet and looked back up at

Gene. "How did he end up in his wheelchair?" I asked.

"Car accident," Gene replied solemnly. The tone in his voice

indicated to me that the news I was about to hear would not be easy to

stomach. My heart raced rapidly as I anxiously waited for his response.

"While Manny was escaping the police, he ran a red light and collided

with another vehicle." Gene took a couple short breaths, as he fell silent for the longest time. He took another deep breath and spoke in an almost

whisper. "The driver Manny collided with was your brother,"

Chapter 9

The words snuck into my mind like a ravenous, filthy weasel, filling my body with malice and spite. A darkness filled my heart as I stared blankly at gene with pursed lips. A scowl formed on my face as my mind began to piece together the clues.

"Why hasn't he been caught yet?" I asked softly trying to keep my anger from erupting. Gene looked at me with his eyes fixated in a way that could only be described as emphatic concern in his eyes.

"Because he has temporal immunity to the law as long as he stays in that forest," my eye twitches as I felt the vein in my neck throb from pulsating blood.

"What you're saying is that while we're stuck here suffering, he walks free of his crimes?" Gene's voice dropped to a whisper as his lip quivered with hesitation.

"Yes, I'm afraid so. The forest is too dense for vehicles to pass through, and to broad to send out law enforcement. The best we can do is drown him out or wait," I couldn't stand to listen to any more. I could feel my heart beating faster I paces back and forth rubbing my chin.

"Thomas, it isn't your place to do anything. If you take matters into your own hands, you could have a record against you. It can ruin your life," Gene said slowly.

"Like they haven't ruined my life already, what more do I have to lose?"

"Your pride. If you do anything rash, you're no better than him,"

I stopped pacing. "You said that the tree line was too narrow for vehicles to pass," I questioned.

"Yeah, what about it," Gene asked cautiously.

"I think I may have an idea, but we will worry about that after the wedding, c'mon it's almost time, and you need to get ready," Gene stared at me blankly for a moment. I could tell he was still processing what I just asked him. Smiling faintly, I gestured him towards the house.

"Move, soldier," he chuckled and saluted me as he marched towards the house. Turning my back to him, I stared at the tree line thinking my plan carefully. I was so fixated in my thoughts that the sound of Lesli's voice made me jump.

"I couldn't help but overhear you and Gene," she began.

"Couldn't help *overhear*, or couldn't help *eavesdrop*?" I smirked.

"A little bit of both," Lesli muttered, "anyways, I want in,"

"I can't risk it, you're too valuable," I muttered under vacant stare.

"Is it because I'm crippled, or is it because I'm a girl," she sneered.

74

"It's neither, it's just that your life is to...your life is too precious to be

tampered with, I must go alone,"

"Then I will tell Gene," she threatened.

"Do you think I really care? Gene isn't my father so he can piss off for all

I care,"

"Like it or not, Thomas, Gene is part of your family! I don't understand

why must you do everything in secrecy?" I stopped scanning my eyes, and

slightly looked up at the sky.

"Because if no one does, then how do we know justice has be served?"

"Revenge is not justice, it's just foolishness," Lesli said looking at the

ground. "If you want to go alone, then I won't stop you. Just answer me

this question: who *are* you, Thomas? What calls you to the forest," I

looked at her with a slight smirk before turning to head into the woods,

leaving her drown in my words:

"More than you could ever imagine."

The soft underbrush crushed under my feet as I ducked under

dangling branches. The rough appendage of the trees elongated fingers felt

wet to the touch as a foul musky odor clung to my hand. Lifting my

fingers to my nostrils. Sniffing the translucent liquid slowly I let out a soft gag as wiped my hands on the britches of my pants.

"Wolf piss," I muttered, "Still warm."

The earth shifted slightly, as a low rumbling rang through my ears.

Turning around, I froze in place as a crippling shiver shot through my

spine. Standing before me was a massive mesh of fur. Shoulder height of

the wolf, was about nine feet with eight inch incisors. Its nose crinkled

with sincere ferocity as its lip curled into a threatening snarl. Its golden

eyes shimmered through dense fur, pointed ears lay back on the wolf's

head as a small bullet hole was surprising distinguishable as it watched me

move away with slight apprehension. The black beast spat silently as the

deep rumble continued to echo through its larynx. The wolf parted its jaws

to run a smooth and pink tongue over their teeth, before a soft but

dangerous unwelcomed intonation dripped through the wolf's tightly

clenched teeth.

"Filthy human, who dares to trespass on to our territory!" The black

lupine questioned hastily. I looked around with admiration and confusion

as the wolf grew impatient. Words flew around my mind like the

scrambler ride at the county fair, I took in a deep breath but all that came

out was "talk". The wolf lowered his head to the ground as he stopped

growling.

"Yes, I do talk, but not very proud of it. Few of us actually speak to humans, but that doesn't explain why you're here, and why I haven't ripped you apart and eaten you," he said licking his teeth again.

"I am looking for a man named Manny, he is a wanted criminal," the wolf sat on his haunches and stared at me with a bit of a suspicious glare.

"Criminal, hardly! The man saved me as well as my sister. Why, he even has me convinced my own brethren dare turn against me. But why am I telling you this, I have spared your life once don't think I will do it again, or you will feel what wrath Wisdom can really do...wait...you've got Athena's scent on your skin, what have you done to her!"
The wolf leapt to his feet, and pounced on me, slamming my body against the dirt.
"Where is my mother?"
"Dead...from battle..."I replied weakly, The black wolfs eyes narrowed into slits as he picked up my body in his jaws and shook me ferociously. My head snapped to and fro at vicious speeds before landing on my side in the hard ground rolling in the dirt, I coughed and held my side as I gasped trying to regain stamina.
"You dare slay a Blackclaw?" He asked snapping his jaws, hunkering his body to the ground ready to strike.

"Wisdom that is enough. He wasn't the one who killed her, Ember was," a voice called from behind. Wisdom turned around as a smaller timber wolf slowly padded towards me. "Stay out of this Fang," he snarled as he licked his teeth from my blood.

"Like it or not, it is the truth. Manny told her to. I've seen it," the timber wolf came around to my side, and sat next to me, licking the dirt from my wounds.

"Athena took a liking to you," Fang said softly, "but wisdom is right, you shouldn't be here it's not safe, if you want to see us, there is an abandoned cottage down the creek that Manny stays away from for obvious reasons since one of them is that it's too close to civilization."

"How do you know all this," I asked. The timber wolf lay on his belly and looked at me.

"Get on, I will tell you at the cottage. These parts are regularly patrolled," looking at Wisdom, he narrowed his eyes and gave a warning bark before trotting into the forest. Black pelt flicking against the brush.

PART 2

Chapter 10

The heavy burden hung slightly in the air as a casket was being lowered into the damp and mucky earth. It was an ill day; a day of grief and consolation. Tears were mixed into the rain as the heavens grieved over a fallen ally. An American flag clung tightly to the polished box as it was lowered to the ground. Suddenly the rope that was lowering the casket snapped as the large wooden box dangled helplessly by a single cord. The casket hatch flew open and the corpse fell out into the hole. Rain continued to fall as the side of the grave walls began to cave in. The truck spun its wheels as mud flew through the air. With a forward jerking motion the cord holding the casket and fell into the hole upside down. The American flag ruined with mud stains and the body crushed under the coffins massive weight. The door to the truck swung open as the driver peered over the gravesite. A heavy hand grabbed him by the shoulder and pulled him back just as more flooded sod filled the disastrous hole.

Gene's eyes narrowed with rage as he pressed the driver up against the truck, teeth grit and nose flared like a bewildered horse.

"That man was a green beret, risking his life so that your sorry fat ass doesn't get deployed and end up like him. All he asked for on his death was a decent burial, and you go and mess it up with your incompetent driving skills," the man against the truck swallowed hard against the furiously, deranged soldier.

"I don't control the weather, mistakes just happen," a fire tormented Genes eyes as he slammed the man against the truck.

"Gene that's enough," a dry voice rang. The soldier's eyes turned to the voice, as a tall man with many badges to his name stood at attention, "Let him go."
Gene stayed where he was, breathing hard as his blood pressure was throbbing in his veins.

"That's an order soldier," the voice rang dryly as it confirmed authority. Gene slammed the man's head against the window leaving a blood stain, as he dropped the body. The authoritative figure glared at him as he walked away. "I want to see you at my quarters at fourteen o'clock to discuss your proper punishment," Gene nodded as he cast his eyes on the driver, stepping over him with slight detest.

Gene sat silently at the desk of General Nathan Grimm. The General's eyes stared darkly at Gene as he lit up a cigar, puffing thick rings out his mouth.

"You're a real asshole at times, Gene, I should have you dishonorably discharged for that stunt you pulled, but I'm not because your vast knowledge and skillful arts have been off the charts for the last several months. Our troops have greatly reduced injury and death has been subsided drastically due to your efforts. Which is why I have a special mission on my mind," Nathan Grimm took another puff of smoke.

"Russia has been dormant for many months and as you know, that is never a good sign. Men have informed me so far that they are or creating some sort of genetically altered warfare that, if deployed will be able to wipe out surrounding countries. Now I normally don't get involved with foreign affairs, but this one's personal, Gene. It seems to me the president of the genetic operation is holding someone hostage until they get what they want, then the hostage will most likely be killed. I need you to this favor for me, Gene," The general looked at the soldier before him as he folded his hands on the table and leaned his gut forward, speaking in a soft whisper.

"I need you to help save my godson, Gene. I haven't seen him since that witch, "Danica" was deported back to Russia. My men has informed me that the boy is still alive, but is being held against his will. This concerns me, because if the Russians do not get what they want he will most likely be killed.

"What is it they are demanding?" Gene asked slowly and suspiciously.

"Manny…..more importantly, a black wolf by the name of Ember. You got to help me, Gene, as your friend, I am begging you…if not for me, then do it for your Thomas' sake…bring his brother home,"

***

Water dripped through the rotted ceiling of the old house that stood in the middle of the forest while Thomas lay on the cold ground, the scuttling of roaches could be heard through the wall. The grey pelted wolf clicked its nails against the expansive dining hall as it made its way to the sink, where it lapped up murky rain water from the sink basin. Thomas looked around and gave a disgusted snort as he listened to the excessive lapping. He walked over to the wolf and peered into the water which consisted of dead leaves, floating bugs, and a few dead mice, he gagged at the smell of the rancid rain water as he looked over his shoulder.

"This place is in ruins," he muttered. Fang gave a soft burp as she licked the water off her jowls.

"Hasn't been active for quite some time, no one knows what happened to the previous owners" she muttered. Thomas sighed with a small shake of his head as he walked around the house. The front foyer from where Thomas came in was small, but evenly spaced. He looked around as he stared breathlessly at the intricate designs on the banister leading up to a small loft that housed a queen sized bed, dresser, night stand, and a balcony that overlooked the forest. Turning around, to his left was a small hallway that lead to the bathroom with bedrooms tucked neatly inside the eroded, moldy drywall. He headed back to the kitchen which was small, but had a spacious fire place in between that separated living from dining.

Thomas let out another sigh as he sat carefully on the sagging couch, expecting mice to jump out from under the cushions, but decided it would probably be best to sit on the floor instead. Fang glanced at Thomas before she rubbed her head on his hair, filling it with a discrete musky scent.

"My siblings know my scent, if you wear it, you cannot be harmed even from Wisdom," a sly smirk slid across his face as he grimaced. Thick residue clung to his hair as he listened to the small patter of rain drip through the cracks of the ceiling. Fang gave a toothy grin as she sat on her belly in front of Thomas, her nose twitching as she panted, biting at her neck "what's the matter, fleas?" Thomas asked.

"Not fleas, it's these darn collars, they are fitted to tight; it's hard to breathe," she coughed. Thomas looked at her questionably as he raised a brow.

'Collar?' he asked. Fang coughed again as her voice grew raspy, almost choking Thomas jumped to his feet, and he raced over to the suffering wolf and dug through her fur. Blood pulsated through his veins as he felt a tight piece of leather wrapped around her neck.

"This material is restricting your airway and it's suffocating you," he murmured. Fang panted deeper as she bit at her neck vigorously.

"Can you get it off?" she gasped. Thomas looked at the leather strap which was nothing more than a leather belt.

"Yeah, I can," he snorted as he worked his fingers around the object. He sighed relief as soon as he got the belt loosened from its choke hold. Fang stood up and shook her heavy pelt as she gasped, and then coughed.

"Thank you," she motioned as she rubbed her muzzle under Thomas' chin, smiling she inhaled as she sighed contently from the fresh air. Thomas smiled a bit as he looked at the belt and tossed it in the garbage. He glanced over at a black image that stood in the door way, before it slowly padded in and shook its pelt free from the rain. Eyes narrowed into slits as it made its way over to the living room before laying down. The door suddenly burst open as Athena's alpha burst through, Thomas glanced up noticing the girl on his back.

"Lesli!" he called in utter shock. Lesli glanced up with bloody eyes that were covered in scars, "what the hell happened?" He asked.

"There has been an attack!" she gasped as she tried to recollect her thoughts. Thomas looked at her, and then at the wolves who focused their attention on the girl.

"Where and who?" Lesli looked up at Thomas with diluted eyes as she gasped for another breath.

"Bachelorette party, was crashed by..." she gulped catching her breath, avoiding eye contact to mask her sincere sorrow. "By a large black wolf, she was looking for something....someone, your mother had perfume on that smelled like your body spray..." Thomas cradled Lesli in his arms as she closed her eyes, blood pooling from her wounds around her eyes, "Your mother was killed trying to protect me," she sobbed. Thomas' heart sank as his feet grew cold, a bitter hatred brewed in the depths of his being as he clenched his fits in rage: the Vagrant Shadow has found a new source of prey—his family.

Chapter 11

The morning rose early as the sun kissed dew brought in a mellow

crispness. Thomas lay in the damp atmosphere, only moving his head

slightly to watch Lesli shiver as she huddle close trying to keep warm. He

sat up and draped his cloak around her, as the cool morning sent

Goosebumps up his arm. The wolves slept soundly, all except for one.

"Wisdom?" He asked walking over to the black lupine that sat on his

haunches, tasking in the sunlight. He glanced over to Thomas as he flared

his nostrils, exhaling old oxygen into a silent sigh. Thomas stood still; not

in fear, but in awe.

"I wanted to apologize for my anger," he muttered. He let out a low

sigh of frustration, before he closed his eyes. Thomas slowly walked over

to him and trace a finger down the wolf's muzzle but withdrew his hand

when wisdom raised a lip threateningly.

"Why do you let him do this to you?" Thomas asked, tucking his

hands in his pockets.

"It's the only affection I get," he muttered, "in *some* sick way it makes

me feel like he still cares for me, and punishes me so I don't get hurt,"

Thomas narrowed his eyes as he boldly stepped in front of Wisdom, holding his black chin in his hands. He could feel saliva drip through his fingers as Wisdom gave an aggravated snarl.

"Stop it! I have had just about enough of your threats. You are better than this! No wolf grows up a man-eater. It's what's ingrained into your head, and if you let him push you around, then you're going to wind up like Ember terrorizing people's lives because you're too afraid to say no. You can easily tear him apart, but you're afraid that if you do, you will die from loneliness. Well you're wrong! You have your siblings—Ember and Fang! You should be roaming free, not caged up like some house pet!" Wisdoms eyes shot up at Thomas' words as Wisdom forcefully knocked him down, staring deep into his eyes, as saliva dripped from his jowls, deep golden eyes cut through his preys' flesh as he panted heavily. Thomas swallowed hard as he closed his eyes. A rough wet tongue swept over his face and cheek as his tail wagged against his flanks. He panted, but kept slobbering the tiny humans face, smiling as he backed away and barked nuzzling a wet nose into his hand.

"No one's stood up to me like that before, it takes guts, and for that you have my respect....and my apologies for the saliva," he chuckled, before he turned his head towards the house. Thomas sat up and flicked his hands free from the silver goop. Wisdom chuckled again as he walked over to Thomas and rubbed his fur over his body, before stepping back. He stepped back, as he turned his head, sniffing the air. Thomas looked at him and sighed.

"What is it?" Wisdom asked, casting eyes on the human.

"I just wish I knew what he was planning so I could stop him."

A soft voice spoke from the house as Lesli sat on Fang's back. The wolf lowered her belly to the ground, as Lesli sat there.

"He's capturing rare wolves and going to turn them into mindless killing machines," Fang's lip curled as she spoke.

"That's what the boxes are for. He put Ember in charge of killing you, which means, she will destroy every last one of your relatives if she has to. Your whole family tree will be obliterated, and the Bravier family will cease to exist," Thomas narrowed his eyes as he stared at the horizon, then stared at the wolves that seemed to be lost in thought. He stared up at Lesli, and exhaled deeply, before he began to speak.

"If she plans on obliterating my family, then I have no choice but to kill her," Thomas said slowly. Everyone's eyes shot up in protest.

"But how, she's a brute! Any attempt would mark as suicide!" Fang whimpered. Wisdom looked at Thomas with deep sincerity.

"She has a point, if you fail, it will be fatal," Thomas paced his ground as he rubbed his chin.

"Challenging Ember will not be that easy, nonetheless killing her. She maybe a monster on the outside, it's not who she is, of wants to be," Thomas turned his head and turned to reveal a medium sized wolf. Its coat reveled in a dark red hue while its muzzle had a strange but uniquely shaded white and gray.

Thomas snorted and then looked at the new wolf.

"My name is Aurora. I am his new prized possession, but managed to escape when he caught wind of a new pup. Even as we speak he is training her to be like Ember—ruthless and without mercy." Thomas stared at Aurora, as he turned his head.

"I've got a plan," he sighed. The wolves synchronously turned their heads as they perked their ears, "If we want to kill Ember, we must first free ourselves from the shadows. The forest is no longer an option to hide. We must reveal what you are to the rest of the world. You are no longer a pet or slave to wicked deeds. You are by your own virtue free as the wind, vicious as you are kind! You are no longer shrouded in fear, but an ally! You ARE a WOLF!" Thomas demanded proudly. The lupines barked in unison as they lifted their heads and howled to the open sky, scattering a

flock of birds from the highest treetops. Thomas looked at the wolves as

he walked next to Wisdom who lay on his belly, exposing his back for

Thomas to mount. He grinned with pleasure as he stepped up to the wolf.

Once mounted, Wisdom headed into the thickets of the lush, wet foliage;

their days of hiding in the shadows have come to an end.

Chapter 12

Warm saliva blinded Thomas momentarily as the large wolfs jowls flapped in the wind, the wolf skimmed through the dense forest with ease as Thomas raised his rear as if he were a   jockey riding towards the finish line. He could hardly believe that he was about to get his revenge for the crimes Manny had committed. He calculated the malicious deeds carefully: one count animal cruelty, one count homicide, one count theft, one count attempted homicide in the first degree, one count..." His thoughts came to a screeching halt as a shiver went down his spine when he realized he was alone.

"Where's Lesli?" he asked with a sense of concern arising. A long howl rang through the forest as Wisdom let a soft aggravated snarl emit from his throat. A heavy burst of speed jolted through the dark wolfs body as he dodged various trees and jumped over numerous fallen obstacles. Thomas' heart sank as he saw a pack of wolves circling their prey snapping and clawing, waiting for instruction to feast. Wisdom let out a deep snarl as he leapt through the air. In doing so, a heavy mass plummeted into Thomas knocking him off his mount. As Thomas hit the ground, he felt his left arm snap in half, screaming in pain and agony as he rolled into a large tree.

Wisdom snarled as he raised his hackles, protectively standing over the

boy. Thomas slowly got up and stumbled towards Lesli, but was quickly

thrown off guard by the same thing that had knocked him off of Wisdom.

He glanced up as he watched malicious red eyes sink back into the

underbrush. Heavy snarls rang out as Fang and Wisdom effortlessly

fought off the others. Snaps of crushing bone echoed through the trees. A

yelp of pain erupted before Fang dropped the body of her attacker.

Wisdom carefully picked up Lesli by her shirt and placed her on Fangs

back giving her a soft nod. Fang returned the nod and disappeared into the

forest, carrying the frail girl away.

Thomas glared darkly at the beast that broke his arm as he circled the

wolf menacingly, with a large stick to only protect him he couldn't help

but feel sorry for the wolf. This wasn't who it was and he knew it.

Lowering his gaze she threw down his weapon, staring deep into the eyes

of the wolf.

"I'm not going to fight you, I'm not like them and neither should you.

Who are you to play God, and what purpose do you possess if you can't

even maintain a docile heart. Are you any better than the man that drives

you from your home?" Thomas asked as he paced gently, holding his limp arm. The wolf stared at him for the longest time as it still let out a low rumbling snarl. Then, almost as if a change of heart had occurred, the wolf stopped snarling and lowered its ears, slowly walking towards Thomas. Ears pinned back, and tail tucked between its legs, it slowly approached sniffing the air. Thomas slowly reached its hand to touch the forehead of the confused animal. Just as skin was about to touch fur, a deep snarl erupted from the vegetation as flash of fur broke the bond, sending the wolf hurdling into a tree.

Dark fur and vicious fangs stood before him as she flicked her teeth over her gums. Hackles raised as a snarl erupted from her throat; with Thomas weak and vulnerable now was the time to strike, but for some reason she didn't. She simply stood her ground; deep red bloodshot eyes penetrating his soul. A burst of pain ripped through her as the red wolf latched its fangs deep into the scruff of the black demons neck. Vicious snarls ensued the dense vegetation as Thomas retreated into the forest. With the wolves running at his side, he looked for an easy advantage. He found a fallen log that was large enough to run across, pain and adrenaline rushing through his body, he ran up the diagonal tree which was propped up at a ninety degree angle. His eyes scanned for the proper moment and then he took the leap of faith. Everything was in slow motion as he fell, but was relieved when his landing was precise; the soft pelt of the running wolf cushioned his fall. He smiled and chuckled as he turned around catching the feeling of wind in his hair— they were homeward bound.

Thomas looked at Lesli as haunting images aroused in his mind. He looked behind him while he ran to catch up beside Aurora. The light gray wolf trotted hastily through the thick forest as he heard the rushing of helicopter blades overhead. A tight knot turned in Thomas' stomach as he felt his blood fill with ice. He knew what would happen when the government got involved, these wolves would cease to exist as many of them would be either shot or experimented on for research which in itself would lead to their utter demise. Thomas exhaled briefly as neared the mouth of the forest, hearing the distinct rumble of military vehicles, he looked at Aurora and shook his head, his heart thumping with anxiety and above all, regret.

"How much time do you think we have?" Thomas asked, placing a soft hand on wolfs fine fur.

"Judging by her lack of compassion, and her nasty temperament, I'd say not very long,"

"I was afraid of that" he murmured looking up to the sky, "I guess it's now or never."

The grey wolf let out a soft whimper as she licked Thomas' hand gently, all the while Lesli remained quiet. She knew that this was going to end terribly and if it was her demise to be buried with the majestic lupine then that is what she had accepted. Speaking softly, she raised her hand and pulled gently on the wolfs scruff which caught Aurora off guard causing her to instinctually snap her head back in self-defense, but quickly shut her muzzle as soon as she saw what had unintentionally harmed Lesli. "Sorry," Lesli murmured, she then looked at Thomas with a sense of determination, echoing through iris of her eyes. "I'll go first, Thomas. I will need your white undershirt and a large stick." Thomas looked up at Lesli in awe as he had never seen this side of her before: usually docile, but never bold. He looked at her then quickly began to undress. The biting flies soon swarmed his skin as his pale, wounded flesh became exposed. He held out the white shirt and Lesli crafted a white flag of surrender from the materials.

Nobody really knows what it's like to walk into friendly fire, because frankly nobody has lived to tell the tale, but for Lesli it was a different kind of feeling—an obligation to protect these animals no matter the cost; even if it lead her to demise. She felt a sort of pride glowing in her, to be mounted on a Belgium-sized gray wolf, holding a staff of surrender, she almost felt like heroine in a movie. Her feet firmly planted at the wolves flanks she grasped the white flag firmly in her hand as she approached the clearing, she looked down at Aurora and whispered in her ear.

"You know what to do," Aurora indeed knew what to do, even though they had not discussed the procedure, she was familiar with the plan: walk into the open and hope that the soldiers as well as Gene saw that they were not here to harm anyone—they just wanted to live around humans in peace. Tilting her head back, Aurora gaped her maw open slightly and howled an eerie moan. Lesli watched from the brush as the men lowered their weapons and looked around trying to determine where the sound was coming from, with no little time to waste, Aurora prodded her way through the brush with Lesli proudly on her back. Lesli waved the white flag, yelling at the top of her lungs:

"Don't shoot! THEY'RE OUR FRIENDS!" Gene glanced up at Lesli and then waved his fingers three times pointing to the forest as other men surrounded the wolf. Aurora let out a protective growl as men attempted to pull her from her mount, while Aurora was distracted, men from all sides threw ropes around Aurora's muzzle, and began to tie it shut. She snarled with such ferocity that she forgot that Lesli was on her back as she began to buck wildly. Then men managed to pull Lesli from her mount as they dragged her off to the paramedic van.

"Check her for wounds, take care of any cuts, scrapes, bite marks this beast may have inflicted" Gene's voice shouted over the ruckus of the snarls coming from Aurora. Being at the disadvantage Lesli was, she was literally helpless. Fierce commands echoed through the commotion as he barked even more orders.

"Infiltrate the forest, seek out and destroy any other mutants you can find!" Gene shouted

a shrilling scream of horror came from Lesli as her heart raced and tears filled her eyes. He turned to the child and briskly walked past her.

"It has to be done," he muttered.

"YOU'RE MONSTER!" She screamed, "HOW COULD YOU DO THIS TO THOMAS AND I?" She bawled, "WE TRUSTED YOU, AND YOU'RE JUST GOING TO LET THEM DIE!"

"Monsters are made, never born you should know that," he said gruffly, as he walked away from the scene, in a few short moments, there was a heartbreaking yelp as Aurora fell victim to humanities cruel act and to the ground her lifeless body fell.

******

Thomas sat upright as he heard footsteps from soldiers approach from all directions, he remained hidden from their sight as he watched their movements. Their stout figures moved carefully from the trees as their guns lay close to their chest, elongated fingers formed a sideways *C* against the trigger of their automatic weapon. He kept a careful watch as he followed their trails distinctly, and when he saw an opening, he made a dash for it. Jumping over brush and fallen pine, his broken arm banged against his side, as he held it with his right hand as he let out a lone howl, warning the wolves to retreat and evacuate the forest. He met up with Wisdom, who was badly injured, but still able to flee on three legs.

"I thought you were dead," Thomas asked, running along the black lupine.

The lupine chortled a little bit, as he hobbled over dense vegetation and kept his nose to the ground picking up unfamiliar scents, keeping his injured leg elevated.

"This way," he barked as he veered to the left. Thomas followed close behind to the best of his ability. Skin scratching against the rough bark of trees left splotches of blood on white pine that reopened cuts that were already almost healed. Wisdom, lifted his head back, sticking his nose to the air, as he looked at Thomas with concern only for a millisecond, then looked back to the trail.

"The pack is regrouping by the waterfall, it's a secluded place so these humans shouldn't be able to find it, and by the time they do we will be long gone..." he went solemn for a moment. "I should add, Ember will be there, when we heard Aurora's dying yelp, we decided it was best not to kill each other, we have bigger threat. She maybe a killer, but we are still a family, and like your family, we have to stick together."

He grumbled a few intangible words, then halted in front of a waterfall where sound of rushing water poured into the lake bed like an overflowing kettle of boiling pasta. Thomas slowly followed Wisdom down into a small gully where the river flowed freely. Through the frigid water, they both entered cavern. Damp and unamused by the choice of location, but it was the only place they could hide. Shaking his damp black coat, Thomas lifted his arms over his face and wrinkled his nose as the smell of wet wolf held prevalent in the secluded cavern. Water dripped from the ceiling as the lupine huddled together for warmth. Thomas looked around at each lupine and noticed that Embers eyes were not as red as they were; granted they still spelled hatred, but for some reason, there was a sense of sorrow behind the bloodshot eyes.

"I gathered you here today, tell you that I am stepping down from Manny's side, and joining Thomas in the fight to bring down his corrupt mind and to end his suffering," Ember began, "This does *NOT* mean that you can rub against me like you are my pup. You are still human and still reek of that human stench, but granted, I realize that too many lives have been lost already, too much suffering has been executed for this to go on; *with* that being said, we must devise a strategic plan to cause the humans to back down and *make* them listen to us, although we cannot speak the tongue they do, Thomas will be our interpreter," Ember licked her muzzles as she bent down for a drink for water that formed by her paws, before speaking again.

"The only reason why Aurora lost her life is because she succumbed to them and assumed that they would go easy on here because she was different than her. NO! Humans fear what they do not understand. If we are going to bring Manny down we are going to be on the same page as them. Right now even as we speak these soldiers are looking to terminate us. That is why we will stay here till nightfall, *then* we will depart. Thomas will ride on my back since Wisdom is too injured to carry any weight, we will follow different trails, so that we can cover our tracks if we are to be pursued. Until then, Layla and Fang will hunt together since they look like each other, they mirror each other's moves that way if they are spotted, they will be able to confuse the humans and retreat until we can send someone else to hunt," The wolves nodded in agreement and looked around before they went to their separate corners to lay down.

"Thomas a word?" Ember asked.

"Of course," he replied as his heart raced. Ember padded out of the cavern as she stood close by the rushing water so that the others could not hear their conversation.

"I don't want you to get any ideas, about you and me. I know that your species killed Aurora, and for that I hold you accountable. I have no desire in getting close to you, but soon as we are done here, if you ever set foot on our territory again I will personally rip you from limb to limb and leave your corpse to rot for the birds to peck at, do I make myself clear?" her voice was cold, and it pierced Thomas in a way no words could have ever done.

"Perfectly." Thomas replied.

"Good," Ember sneered.

Chapter 13

Darkness finally settled amongst the land. Thomas sat up as the lupine he was resting on became restless. Thomas yawned as his eyes adjusted to the night, the pale moonlight illuminated the pond below the waterfall as he followed the light into the open air. The ambient forest was filled with the chorus of song. Critters called to one another, just as insects buzzed merrily through the night echo. A yowl of a cougar in the distance silenced the critters as the air suddenly became still. Ember sat on her haunches and stared at each member closely; her black fur rippled as she paced back and forth.

"The plan is simple," she stated justly. "We divert, distract, and deliver. Fang and Layla will divert anyone off the path. These humans are persistent so there is bound to be some stragglers. Wisdom will distract along the help of Flame. Thomas, myself, and Tristan will deliver the message. If all else fails we will conspire at dawn and surround them, hopefully we won't have to revert to that plan but if nothing else works, we have a backup plan," The wolves seemed to understand and barked in agreement. Thomas nodded in agreement as well.

"Thomas you go with Tristan, I have mattered to attend to," Ember said briskly. Thomas opened his mouth to speak, but Ember cut him off before he could say a word.

"If you want to keep your vocal chords, I would advise not to argue and *just* do it," Ember growled as she leapt to her feet. "Remember the plan, stick together," they all barked as she left her sanctuary.
Tristan pushed a wet nose into Thomas' hand as she looked into his eyes. Her golden iris softened and let out a soft whine.

"Don't worry about her, she has always been that way," She panted as she leaned her body against Thomas' arm.

"I know, Tris. I just worry about her sanity," Tristan cocked her head to the side.

"Well, she *is* alpha—Manny made her that way, so with that power she has to live up to her stature,"
Thomas rubbed the wolfs' fur as she moaned with delight. He looked ahead as he saw the edge of the clearing where the forest ended. Stopping briefly, he looked around before proceeding.

"I will go ahead, but keep your distance," He instructed. Tristan whined a bit, then nodded

"Alright, but be careful," she said stroking a soft tongue against the grain of Thomas' wrist. Thomas smiled faintly at the affection and exited the thickets, heading across the lawn towards the house.

He reached the front door and turned the handle as he me made his way inside. Things were suspiciously quiet. *Where is everyone?* He kicked off his shoes and crept through the house as he felt an odd sense of trepidation. *Where is Max?* He questioned silently. A shiver went down his spine as he glanced at the pictures in the frames—they were all blank. *The hell?* Thomas looked around as the room begun to spin, and the daylight of an early morning broke his dream transferring him back to the mortal realm.

Thomas sat up and propped his elbows against the fur of the sleeping lupine. As the wolves began to stir, waking up slowly opening their maws to reveal their to reveal six inch incisors pale, elongated tongues that curled under their gums and razor sharp teeth that lined the inside of the gums. Thomas looked around as he counted heads noting their leader was missing. He felt warm arms wrap around him as a body pulled themselves closer.

"Good morning," a voice whispered as he felt the embrace tighten. He blinked and looked at Lesli who was slowly waking up; her eyes grew wide when she saw who she was cuddling.

"Thomas!" she gasped as a bright blushed filled her pale cheeks.

"What are you doing here?" he asked

"Well…I *was* sleeping," she mumbled, yawning, curling up again to go back to sleep. Thomas sat and listened to the forest. Thomas' body began to tense as he listened closely trying to isolate the ambience of the forest, in the distance he could heard men shouting directions. His body froze still as the wolves looked around becoming tentative, careful not to make a sound.

"Lesli! Wake up, we have to go!" he said getting up abruptly, the wolves stood up quickly becoming more attentive to the noise.

"Something wrong?" Tristan asked as she yawned again, stretching her legs.

"Humans," Ember snorted. "Not just *any* humans…Search and Rescue— the humans aren't alone, they have Irish wolf hounds," her lip curled angrily, "Layla, Fang, wake up!" She barked, "We've got company! I need you to divert them! "Wisdom, go with Flame to keep them occupied. Lesli and Thomas you come with me, I will carry the girl!" Ember ordered briskly. Thomas nodded and placed Lesli on Ember's back looking back at Tristan.

"I will deliver Lesli to the house, Thomas see if you can get to Geno in one piece." She snarled. Thomas nodded in understanding. In a single bound, Ember plowed out of the cavern as Thomas and Tristan remained in her wake.

"We have to go find Gene and tell him to call them off!" Thomas stated.

Tristan barked as she bowed her front paws to the ground which indicated for Thomas to climb on; in a hasty jump Thomas mounted the silver lupine as she too bounded off into the foliage.

Chapter 14

The rich, green foliage brushed against Thomas' leg as he held it tightly against the lupines side. The powerful muscle rippled through the animals' body as soft panting and the snapping of twigs underneath the heavy paws. Thomas ducked his head under a low branch that could have easily decapitated him. The wolf came to a stop as he glanced around, looking for Lesli then, he spotted her: blond hair disheveled amongst the lush green grass, her skirt torn and her legs covered in bruises. Thomas watched as one of his buddies lifted Lesli off the ground and carried her into the house.

What happened he wondered, as he watched with interest? *Was this part a scheme too?* Thomas cast his eyes across the yard as he watched deep red eyes stare at the girl for a moment before retreating into the underbrush, it wasn't until a few moments after that he realized how dangerous it was for the wolves. Even though Gene's buddies were compassionate towards females, they could care less about other people. They would shoot their own kin if they had the chance. They hunted wolves for pleasure and justified their means through "self-defense" As Thomas recalled, Lesli once told him: "there isn't a soft bone in their body. If I had to label them

I would stamp them as *Army Thugs*

Thomas dismounted from the wolf as he took a deep breath and slowly walked towards the house. He looked back at Tristan who began to follow him, but he put a hand to say "stay" she stepped back into the brush. He reached the front porch and walked up the steps allowing himself into the house, closing the door with a soft *click*. Gene was sitting in the living room, tending to Lesli as he opened his mouth to speak.

"Do you know how this happened?" he spoke coldly

"No," Thomas replied.

"You should have taken better care of her," he remarked acidly.

"Maybe *you* should a better *FATHER* and care of her instead of dumping her on the porch like a defenseless puppy!" Thomas seethed. There was a moment of dead silence as he watched Gene wring out the dirty water from the rag, Thomas' heart pumped ferociously as he licked his chapped lips, then calmly and coldly, he added, "Instead of hanging with those heartless delinquents… *Why* are they here, Gene?" The stagnant air fumed with animosity as he put down the rag and turned towards Thomas, eyes filled with scorn and loath. He slowly turned around and exhaled deeply as he applied a bandage to Lesli.

"I got assigned to a mission," He began.

"Yeah, and how does that involve me?" Thomas asked unamused.

"We need your help taking down Manny,"

"Manny, what does he have to do with the mission?"

"Manny has been acting as a double agent. He has been working with Russia to bring the wolves from Timber Falls overseas to breed with the wolves over there so that they may take over surrounding territories. His latest experiment, as you called her the "Vagrant Shadow:" has been the product of genetic alteration that Russian scientists have been working on for years, they have been smuggling this drug…..this….this….devastating injection across the border. Everything we know about Manny is a lie. He didn't lose his ability to walk due to a car crash… they were snapped in half when he failed to comply with orders from his boss. I've been hunting with him for the wrong reasons. Here I thought I was setting traps for catching game when in reality he was using them for catching wolves," He took a breath before he looked at Thomas again.

"There *is* another thing," He began. Thomas looked at Gene with concern, "There is conspiracy that your brother is in fact…. alive."

Chapter 15

A bolt of shock and disbelief rippled through Thomas' body, temporarily crippling him as he looked at Gene for a while.

"I'm sorry, run that by me again?" He stammered.

"Your brother is alive and being held hostage," Thomas felt sick as he fought every effort to vomit from distress.

"So why is this a big cover-up? Why bring *my* family into this…this…scheme?"

"Because Brandon was the only one who could give valuable information about the wolves and the forest. He was the only one who could communicate to the wolves in their own tongue and be able to translate to human speech to them—a rare gift, a phenomenal gift at best. It why he has been able to survive so long. I needed you to help me with this mission to bring Manny down. I wasn't going to let my men get killed by those vicious animals, I needed to lure you out."

"So this was all a trap?"

"You have to understand Thomas, that you've been playing cat and mouse with the law for way too long. You knew it would be only a matter of time before prosecution caught up to you,"

"What prosecution?"

"Obstruction of justice, disorderly conduct, resisting arrest, speeding, attempted vehicular homicide," Gene counted off on his fingers. Thomas scoffed as he looked at him, not able to believe what he was hearing. His mouth grew dry as he looked around. He was going to take the fall for the death of a police officer that he had no part of doing.

"However, Flora talked to the D.A, and if you agreed to help us bring Manny down, we will drop the charges to a first offense misdemeanor, which means you don't go to jail *if* you put in seven hundred hours of community service, and you can choose which service you do as long as its beneficial to your health and community," Thomas felt sick as he looked at Gene.

"Since I have no other choice I will do it. *However,* we do it *my* way because we have allies on our side." It wasn't long before Lesli was back to her old self. When Thomas asked what happened, she said that she fell off her mount when Ember tripped over a tree root that was sticking out of the ground—it was quite ironic that a wolf that lived her life in the forest still was able to be beaten by a tree.

Thomas sat at the counter with a piece of paper in front of him as he mapped out a strategy plan of defense.

"Where is Aunt Flora?" he inquired, realizing he had not seen his aunt for quite some time.

"She is working with the Feds to decipher an encrypted message that the CIA intercepted this morning," Gene explained.

"How is working with the CIA going to help?" he asked. Gene sighed and shook his head.

"Thomas, Manny is a global threat. Who *knows* what Intel he is feeding these foreigners. He could be supplying information about our government that can bring us to anarchy," Thomas stared at the paper for a while then finally spoke after a few moments of processing.

"I am going to need a cargo plane," He states simply, "filled with supplies. Since Manny wants this black wolf so bad, I figure we'd bring her with as a diversion while we grab my brother."

"Whoa, Whoa, Whoa" one of Gene's buddies jumped in, we are *NOT* bringing that *thing* on a plane for *thirteen* hours. We don't even know the temperament, nonetheless the condition of being confined to close quarters for a long period of time. Gene looked at Thomas and shook his head.

"Chip is right, how do we know it won't turn on us mid-flight?"

"Because it...excuse me...*she* wants to bring Manny down as much as *we* do. Besides we will be safe guarded by the other pack members," Thomas explained coolly

"No, freaking way! We are *NOT* bringing a pack of genetically altered wolves on a cargo jet. No way, no how!" Chip argued with sincere disgust.

Thomas looked up from his paper he was studying as he surveyed the group of people.

"Look, I know you're all concerned for safety but we don't have a choice," Thomas pleaded.

"We do *have* a choice. We have the choice of knocking down doors and kicking some hostile Russian mercenary ass." Thomas sighed deeply as he shook his head in frustration, clenching his fists, he pounded the countertop causing his wrists to throb in pain.

"Thomas, where are you going?" Gene asked.

"To cool off," he yelled back slamming the door on the way out. Thomas headed down the wooded steps trudging rapidly through the lush grass not paying attention to anything. His thoughts clouded with aggravation that he didn't even hear his name being called.

"Thomas!" Lesli called. The deranged boy looked behind him as he stopped mid-stride to watch Lesli roll towards him in her all terrain wheelchair, "Where are you going?"

"I already told you, I am going to cool off, and I need time to think."
he said nastily.

"I don't blame you for being angry, but what if the men are right? It's
a long flight. Think of the wolves: cramped space, insufficient oxygen,
limited bathroom breaks, scarce food, heavy turbulence, it's a recipe for
disaster, it's not worth the risk,"

"Look, the military spends *millions* of dollars to carry heavy tanks
over to third-world countries, I don't see how using it to carry a bunch of
allied wolves overseas to help us. I don't even care if these *brutes* want to
act like pansies—the fact of the matter is I am going to save *my* brother."
"That's different Thomas, besides you don't even know if he's alive,"
Lesli whined.

"They will keep him alive as long as they get their precious
prototype," Lesli sighed just as the patio door opened and Gene stepped
out for a light up a cigarette.

"I couldn't help but overhear your bickering. I admire your sense of
enthusiasm and adventurous spirit...*IF* we will go along with your plan
there is to be one condition: Anything happens on that plane....if any of
my men get injured or killed, I am holding you accountable...I will not

hesitate to kill one of them, is that understood?" Gene declared as he puffed out a stream of smoke. Thomas looked at Gene with concern before he opened his mouth to speak.

"Perfectly, *however*, if one of your buddies does anything to provoke the wolf, I *won't* be held accountable. Do I make *myself* perfectly clear?" The air was filled with tense silence as Gene puffed out another stream of smoke and blew it up into the sky.

"No promises," he said, "but I will get on the phone with the general,"

"Then I can't make any promises either," Thomas said. Gene finished his cigarette and went back into the house. His voice booming through the open windows.

"Listen up, ladies here is what's going down. We are going go along with Thomas' plan because we need his expertise on working with genetic wolves. Which means Chip, you are to keep your mouth shut, if you get attacked on that plane I don't want you bitching, do I make myself understood…I don't care what your excuse is, you are going to follow orders or you are going to stay behind, is that *understood*…good!"

Chapter 16

The whirling of airplane blades sent hurricanes of gust through the trees as Thomas set his luggage bag down. The tail of the cargo plane lowered as grinding gears crunched together revealing the insides of the plane. A heavy metal *thunk* sounded as the gears ceased their grinding. The blades slowly died down as the pilot cut off the engine. Thomas looked at Gene who was staring off into the woods.

"You said they would be here." he snarled softly.

"Patience," Thomas muttered.

"You seem to forget that this *is* a rescue mission?"

"Nobody said I forgot," Thomas mumbled.

"Exactly what *is* the plan again? It doesn't make sense," Gene asked for the fifth time now. Thomas rolled his eyes as he repeated the plan of action he had in store.

"We use Ember as bait to lure Manny into the plane. Once he is inside we fasten his wheels to the hooks hanging on the wall. Once he realizes what is going on, it will already be too late. The other wolves will be hiding under a cargo net. Once we land we will release Manny, and he will take her to this…bad guy which I named 'Permafrost'. Meanwhile, as Ember is taking Manny to his boss, she will shed her fur on nearby trees to give us a

trail to follow," Thomas explained, "from there we will infiltrate the

location, rescue Brandon, and dispose of any rogue survivors."

"...*and* Ember is aware of this,"

"She is up to par with this, yes,"

"Are you sure?" Gene questioned. Thomas exhaled a sigh of

frustration.

"Yes but I will go over it again,"

"What of Manny? Won't he be suspicious,"

"Let's hope not," Thomas said softly. Gene sighed and shook his

head, not enjoying the enthusiasm that Thomas was displaying.

"You're responsible," he reminded.

"Yeah, I know."

An unusual rustle stirred from the brush as heads turned to look

up at the wolves emerge from the foliage: Wisdom, Layla, Fang, Flame,

and even Tristan came bounding out of the brush. They looked at the

soldiers wearily, before heading into the plane single file. When they

entered vehicle, Thomas ushered them to the front of the plane where they

nestled themselves together, Thomas then proceeded to create a barrier

using a heavy cargo net. Thomas looked around making sure there were enough hooks to Manny in place. He peeked out from behind the fortress

he made and watched as Lesli hooked her wheelchair up with the red

safety hooks and crawled her way towards the front of the plane.

"Do you think it will work?" Lesli asked, her lip quivered with

uncertainty.

"Nothing can be certain, Lesli, my mind is mapped differently than I

originally anticipate. Let's just pray Ember knows what she is doing,"

"I just hope…" Lesli stopped talking as she gave a small quiet yelp of

surprise as she turned to face Tristan who gently dug her teeth into Lesli's

flesh; it wasn't enough to draw blood but enough to keep her quiet.

Thomas watched carefully as Ember emerged at the tail of the plane with

Manny grasped firmly in her jaws. She swung her head and threw Manny.

Just like a ragdoll Manny flew through the air, before hitting the metal

floor with a powerful *thud* that echoed throughout the cabin. He rolled for

a little bit then was still. Ember stepped over him, and gave the man a

final kick with her back paws.

"Whoops," she snorted sarcastically. She walked to the darkest corner

of the plane and lay down watching with piercing bloodshot eyes glowing

like infrared lights. Gene gave the signal to the pilot and the jet revved up

its engine as it sprang to life. Strong, bulky arms thrust Manny's frame into the chair and hooked his wheels to the large cargo hooks. While they strapped him in securely, Thomas cautiously stepped out from the mesh fortress as he looked at the pitiful state of "man", just like the figure he saw in his dreams.

"Are we ready?" Thomas asked growing impatient.

"Just waiting on Gene," one soldier replied shifting in his seat watching the tail of the plane. It wasn't long before Gene entered the vessel and the back hatch closed as the plane lifted off the ground. Gene looked around at the group then spoke softly.

"I just talked to the pilot. The quickest route we are taking is going to be from Oregon to Alaska. There we will refuel and you can let the *dogs* do their "thing" then from there we set a straight course to Chernobyl." A slight snarl erupted when Gene mentioned the word 'dogs' as Thomas looked at the men who sat on the bench each one hunched over with their head hanging low while they stared at the metal floor.

Thomas' eyes shot up as he looked worried for a moment.

"Chernobyl? That place is condemned. We can't go there! It's walking into a deathtrap! The radioactivity could kill us!"

"Thomas, relax, we have all the gear that we need. As long as you don't dig in the dirt, the radioactivity won't harm you. Besides, I can see why

Manny's boss is so interested in this operation: by using radioactive wolves with this….injection that they created, they would be able to obliterate surrounding countries, plus with the country being condemned there is no one around to question his motives, which makes me wonder…how did he get past the military..?" Gene shook his head and looked at Thomas. "Ah, well, since we are going to be on this trip, I might as well introduce you to my buddies," Gene started. Thomas glared at them.

"You mean *thugs*?" Thomas sneered. One of the soldiers began to get up, but Gene held out his arm in place.

"It's alright, I deserved that." Gene said glancing at the brute soldier as Thomas snorted and rolled his head back sarcastically, "Anyways, the brute is Chip; he's in charge of combat and weapon arsenal. Next to him is Riley, he's a paramedic, and finally we have Sergeant Dawson he's in charge of Geographic Coordination, and well, you know me, I am charge of Negotiation as well as Search and Rescue," Gene gave a soft smile. Thomas sneered as he dipped his head slightly.

"Pleasure. I am Thomas, the black wolf over there with the bloodshot eyes is Ember. The others behind the mesh wall are Tristan, Wisdom, Fang, Flame, and Layla," He explained briefly. He studied the faces of the men for a brief moment then turned his attention to Manny who appeared to be sleeping. Thomas shook his head and walked to Ember who lifted her lip to give a little snarl at his presence.

"Easy, Ember," Thomas said softly. Her expression softened as her lip lowered and she became suddenly sullen.

"The sooner we arrive the sooner I can get rid of that parasite," she mumbled Thomas found a seat and sat close to her.

"What happened?" he inquired.

"Too many unmentionables to explain," she replied quietly.

"What do you mean?"

"He took my innocence," She whispered.

"You mean…" Thomas asked as he moved closer to her.

"Yes, Thomas, I was taken advantage of." Thomas shuddered at the thought of such a vile act as he turned his head and looked at her, reaching a hand to put on her fur. She didn't snap or snarl, but simply looked at him, and licked his hand in confidence.

"But….why?" Ember sighed and looked away as he told the story. "He said he needed the fluid for an experiment he was conducting then tried to put a tracing chip in my "area" When refused he got mad and scalded my hide with a branding iron. I swiped at him and he hit the support beam and fell to the ground. That's when I picked him up in my

jaws and brought him here. Disgusted that such a creature has such a

provocative desire." Thomas looked over at the man slumped in the chair.

"Hey Riley, can you check on Manny to make sure he is still alive?"

"Why wouldn't he be?" Riley asked standing up and walking over to

Manny.

"Please, just do it." Riley exhaled and pressed his two fingers against

Manny's throat and his wrist.

"Yeah, he still is, but judging by the condition and the way he moves,

he's going to have one hell of a backache, and possibly head trauma due

to a blunt force."

"Anyway to treat the condition?" Thomas asked.

"Strap his head in with a belt to keep it from moving or possibly

laying it against something soft." Thomas looked at Ember.

"No, way!" She snarled raising a lip of jagged teeth, "I will just end

his pathetic life; its best he stays where he is." Thomas glanced at Gene

who was rummaging around the plane, where he found a stretcher.

"Thomas I think this stretcher would work better. We carry a lot of

equipment in here some stuff that you would least expect to find," Gene

wheeled the gurney over to where Manny was sitting,

"Plus it would be easier if he was laying down to keep him safe," Riley added. Thomas sighed as they pushed the wheelchair out of the way replacing it with the stretcher. Thomas pressed his foot on the lever near the wheels to lock the bedded gurney. Strapping him in place, they hooked up the legs of the gurney to the wall to make sure it didn't budge. Thomas shook his head in disgust as he watched the man lay comfortably in the elevated stretcher.

"Don't worry, he's going to get what's coming to him," Gene assured, putting a hand on Thomas' shoulder.

Chapter 17

The flight was smooth and calm with very little turbulence. The wolves slept soundly as Thomas paced about the cabin while Riley took vitals from Manny.

"Good news, doesn't seem like Manny has a concussion," Thomas stopped pacing and glanced over at Riley with interest.

"How can you tell?"

"Well normally, concussions are due to inflammation of the brain; had he gotten a concussion, his skull would have swelled, but I am just going off of observation,"

"So we don't know for sure," Thomas asked.

"Not without proper equipment, we need to a brain scan," Riley admitted. Thomas grunted in frustration.

"*Some* paramedic," he mumbled.

"Hey, I am only an intern," Riley stated. Thomas threw his hands up in the air with sarcastic emphasis.

"*Well then* that makes everything *so much* better," he retorted.

"Guys can we not fight right now, please?" Gene asked softly.

"Stay out of this Gene, just remember you're the one who brought these hooligans with you!"

"*Hooligans*!" Chip exclaimed. "We've got more courage than you and your mutts combined. While you're shooting up heroine, we're shooting up bad guys to make sure you can still have your freedom!"

"I *don't* shoot up heroine," Thomas mumbled. Chip bull snorted and gave a glare.

"Sure you don't kid, I've worked with Riley long enough to see the symptoms: pale skin, droopy, blood-shot eyes, I wouldn't be surprised if you shot up with Ember. That's why she's the way she is," His voice trailed off as a ferocious snarl caught him off guard, echoing through the cabin as Chip was tackled to the ground by a black force. Thomas looked around at the figure and distinguished the figure by their bitten ear lobe.

"Wisdom, STOP!" Thomas yelled but before anyone could react, a gun shot rang out and Wisdom fell on his side. An angry roar rang through the plane as Thomas knelt beside the dead lupine. His hands grasped the fur of Wisdom's thick fur coat; adrenaline pumping through Thomas' veins as bewildered eyes locked on to Chip.

"What did you do?" Thomas asked, his voice cracked with anger and sorrow as his heart began to beat faster.

"Self-defense," Chips shrugged.

"Bullshit! You…." Thomas stammered.

"I'm what….right?" Chip smirked. Thomas gulped as his throat grew dry and he tried his best to swallow, but felt like he was suffocating.

"Since you killed Wisdom, you can die too," Thomas growled softly. Chip chuckled softly and gave a smirk.

"I would like to see *you* try," Gene got up and stood between them. "Thomas, I warned you about this…..let it go," Thomas looked at Gene with diluted, tear-filled eyes.

"Piss off Gene, you're a bigger asshole for being so blind by your own arrogance. What happened to your sense of compassion?"
"I know you are upset, but don't do anything stupid, just think it through," He begged.

"Move, Gene this doesn't concern you,"
"Actually, *it does*, Thomas, we talked about this, remember: *no promises*" he began as he walked away slowly.

"Oh, I thought it through alright," he growled as he punched an emergency red button on the wall. Red lights flashed as the floor began to open, dumping the cargo. The atmospheric vacuum was immense, it created a massive vortex through the cabin. As the red light flashed the pilot's voice on the intercom was drowned out by the gusting winds as Wisdom's body was sucked down the chute and thrown into the wind as his body tumbled down limply to the ocean below. The red light continued to flash as the door closed cutting off the vortex.

"Nice work, *Tom*." Chip sneered. Gene clenched his fists and gave Chip a solid punch to the face, causing Chip's nose and lip to bleed.

"You stupid ass, we just lost an ally! We were going to use him to navigate through the terrain and now we are down by *one*," Gene spat. "You can walk your happy ass through the snow for all I care." Thomas gave a small look at Chip as Chip wiped the blood off his swollen lip and nose. A voice flashed over the intercom as Thomas went to sit back down.

"The hell is going on back there, I nearly clipped a wing....Never mind, don't tell me, I don't want to hear it. Any more problems and we are aborting this mission I am not risking my life just so you guys can act like idiots," the intercom clicked off and the cabin fell silent as Thomas sat by Ember looking at her sympathetically.

"I am so sorry," He whispered.

"Don't be. Wisdom has always been reckless despite his name,"

A hard *thud* resonated as the plane bounced along the runway.

Thomas held onto whatever was available until the plane came to a complete stop, Thomas slid off his seat as the plane fishtailed before coming to a complete halt, as the pilot pulled into the fueling station the wolves stretched while the planes hatch dropped to the ground. The wolves slowly walked out of the plane and into the crisp Alaskan air, sniffing the unfamiliar scents. Ember followed behind sullenly as she glared at Chip who was taking a smoke break off into the distance. Silently, Ember crept up behind Chip, and raised her hackles. Saliva dripped from her fangs as she licked them menacingly; before Chip could even note what was happening, Ember had his head in her jaws—severed from the rest of the body. Ember quickly disposed of the body and trotted back to the plane and slunk into the shadows and waited for everyone's return. When everyone returned, they were surprised to see that Chip was longer among them. His body was found over the edge of a cliff as Gene peered over the ledge.

"There is no way he could have survived that," he stated obviously.

"No one saw what happened; he must have taken a wrong step," Dawson said.

As obedient as domestic dogs, the wolves came out of the forest and boarded the plane not taking a second glance at the others. Thomas boarded lastly and sat next to Ember, a sense of scrutiny seemed to hang about her.

"Ember…?" Thomas began his serious tone in his voice.

"I killed him," She muttered. Thomas gaped his mouth open, "Don't patronize me human, you know the rules," she snarled. Thomas looked at her and shook his head before moving to the back of the cargo net where Lesli slept soundly. Flame lifted his head to look at him and whimpered softly laying his head in Thomas' lap.

"We all knew it would come to this," Flame said softly. Thomas looked at him and stroked his fur gently.

"Yeah, I know," He muttered, slumping on Tristan's side and falling asleep into her warm fur.

Chapter 18

The remaining flight was long and uneventful. The wolves neither barked nor quarreled; it was for once, peaceful with a subtle undertone. The plane bounced along the runway as the aircraft pulled into a military hangar.

"We're here," the Pilot said.

"Good." Gene sighed softly, "Manny is waking up." Ember huffed as she got into position slowly trotting to Manny's side obediently laying down. Gene unstrapped him from the stretcher and put him into the wheelchair as he was slowly coming too.

"What….the hell is going on?" He demanded.

"You had an accident. Your boss wanted to make sure you brought the mutt to him in one piece so he asked me to accompany you." Gene looked at him sincerely.

"Fine, whatever," Manny groaned as he slumped in his chair. Gene wheeled the crippled man down the ramp as Ember followed right by his side. Once off the plane, and into the frigid air, Ember knelt down so Manny could climb on to her back with the help of Gene.

"What about the boy?" Gene asked casually.

"I don't know. The boss isn't known for keeping promises." Lesli shot

Thomas a glance of concern as they listened to the conversation.

"You *did* come alone, right?" Manny asked. Gene scoffed and laughed nervously.

"Of course, we can't fit a mutt this size on a commercial liner without drawing attention." Manny nodded as he seemed pleased with Gene's response.

"Yes, that would be *fatal*," Manny stated looking ahead of him. Looking back at Gene one last time he squeezed his legs against the wolf's sides with his prosthetic legs.

"Let's go." Ember snorted with disgust as she moved her legs, walking into the woods before she broke into a powerful stride. With each tree she passed she rubbed her flank against the bark, marking her trail. Once Ember was out of view, Thomas slowly exited the aircraft carrying Lesli in his arms. With the wolves closely by their side, he placed Lesli on the back of Flame while he mounted Tristan. Fang and Layla synchronously lowered their bodies to the ground as Riley and Dawson anxiously mounted the wild lupines fur.

"So, here's the plan: we follow Ember as far away as possible, but still keeping tabs on her whereabouts. When we get close to our destination, I want Riley to take out any rooftop mercenaries. Dawson, will go and throw a flash grenade, while they are temporarily blinded, I will infiltrate the hideout and rescue Brandon, but we must leave Manny alive." Lesli shifted her weight as the bitter cold stung her cheeks.

"You sure this will work?" She asked.

"Nothing is for sure, but nothing is granted without trial," Riley finished for Thomas as he looked at Thomas nervously, "Never did ride a wolf before."

"Don't get used to it. It's just this once," Thomas sneered. Tristan looked at Thomas and nipped his leg gently. He smiled faintly at Tristan who was trying to tell him. *"Don't get cocky,"*

"Let's get moving," Dawson instructed. He gently tapped the animals' side and headed towards the forest as he clicked his tongue. Hearing the command, the wolf perked its ears and sprung into the forest. They traveled for what seems like an eternity with noses pressed to the ground; with the scents on the trees the wolves spread out as they prepared the assault. They came to a halt and looked around confused.

"What happened to the trail?" Tristan questioned.

"I don't know," Flame replied sticking up in the air sniffing. His eyes gazed around as his nose led him to a familiar scent.

"There!" He called bounding towards an abandoned cabin.

"Keep a look out, this place could be wired," Thomas motioned quietly. The wolves spread out once more as each one took a corner of the house. Thomas slowly dismounted and stepped carefully next to his ride. Riley and Dawson did the same. Flame lead Lesli into the thickets of the brush as the wolves ran freely to surround the cabin. Thomas stealthily crept to the windows crouching down, listening to the conversation. The man had a heavy accent and a distinct dialect which made it hard to understand.

"You got the prototype, yes?"

"Yes sir, I got her chained up around back,"

"You did well, Vlad." The man nodded once and one of the henchmen went out back to retrieve Ember. A disgruntled groan and muffled *snap* of a neck could be heard as Thomas saw Gene dress himself as the henchman, and bring Ember into the cabin. With the rescue set in motion, Thomas carefully crawled towards Gene's gear and rummaged through the supplies which included: bulletproof vest, .9 MM handgun, frag grenades, flash grenades (also known as stun grenades), helmet, ammunition, etc. Thomas carefully looked over the supplies, and pocketed a flash grenade as he continued to listen on the conversation.

"Your liege if I may speak," Manny began.

"Yes, what is it Vlad?"

"I was just asking about payment for my services,"

"We had a deal: you get the kid as your apprentice and I get the wolf who has a very busy schedule of mating." Thomas gasped softly as he bit his lip thinking about what was happening.

"Ember is a sex slave?" he questioned quietly.

"Manny, stand up, you don't have to pretend anymore; we all know you're not really crippled," the boss said in a dark and almost sinister tone. Manny rose out of the wheel chair that was presented to him as he walked over to the malicious leader, standing close range. The leader walked around Manny and inspected him with curious and sinister admiration.

"You wouldn't lie to me, now would you, Manny?" Manny licked his chapped lips nervously as he watched the man circle him.

"Of course not, my liege," Manny responded nervously. Thomas heart raced as he kept low profile beneath the windowsill.

"Then maybe you can tell me how you would explain *THIS!*" The ruthless leader pulled the hood back that Gene was wearing exposing his face and neck. A burst of panic shot through Manny as he watched in horror.

"I swear I had nothing to do with that," he pleaded. Permafrost gave a subtle nod of pseudo-sympathy as the person standing behind Manny crept up behind him and swung a metal bat against Manny's calf muscles. The poor man let out a scream of pain as a sharp *crack* in the bones could be heard, and Manny felt to his knees bowing before his ruler. Permafrost placed a heavy boot on Manny's skull as he pressed his face into the cold, ground.

"The deal is off, I thank you for bringing me the wolf, but it seems like you won't be getting your payment. The only price you will be paying is with your life; but don't worry you will be   joining Brandon," He turned his attention to the henchmen and gave a small nod

"Kill them both." Thomas' eyes widened as he heard the command.

"No!" Thomas yelled as he pulled the pin to the flash grenade and chucked it through the broken window. A burst of blinding white powder erupted from the canister as it filled the room, as Ember broke free from the metal chain and shackles that bound her. The shackles around her ankles jingled as she scooped up Brandon in her jaws and broke down the door Thomas jumped through the window and threw Gene the gun who had just elbowed one of Permafrost's henchmen in the gut.

Gene took cover as he caught the gun in one hand and opened fire; rounds rang out as shells it the floor. The other wolves broke through the house just as the smoke was beginning to clear releasing feral monstrosity upon the unsuspecting henchmen.

Thomas picked up Manny by the scruff of his cloak and dragged him out the door, bone showing through the pale skin; Thomas rushed out of the cabin while gun fire continued to ring. He hoisted the man on to Flame's back as he turned his head to the wolf.

"Take him to the plane!" He instructed hastily as Riley and Dawson followed beside the surviving men who were escaped on snow mobiles to pursue Ember.

Powerful strides broke the silence as muscular legs from Fang and Layla broke through the forests vast vegetation. It wasn't long before the wolves caught up to the snow mobiles who maneuvered effortlessly through the frozen forests' maze; with a powerful burst of speed Layla

jumped over the snow mobile and barricaded the men's path, barring sharp teeth as she unlocked her jaw and opened her mouth, ready to have an easy meal. The man squeezed the brake so hard that the force of impact caused him to fly off his snowmobile and into the jaws of Layla who snapped his back before swallowing the body in one bite.

It wasn't long before Fang caught up to the other snow mobile, and pulled the man off his ride from behind, causing the vehicle to swerve out of control and crash over a cliff. Tristan and Thomas followed in hot pursuit of the final member of Permafrost's clan reaching speeds of forty to fifty miles an hour. While running alongside of the snow mobile, Thomas slowly stood on Tristan's back and balanced himself briefly before taking a leap and tackling the man, knocking the man to the ground. The vehicle spun out of control and crashed into a tree, exploding on impact.

Ember looked behind her in a quick glance as she continued to hold Brandon in her jaws. When she saw what was ahead of her, she only had a few seconds to react: she tossed her head and threw Brandon into the snow as she slid on slick ice towards the edge of a cliff, as she tried to stop, but it was no use. Her body was violently was thrown over the ledge; bone chilling yelp of demise echoed through the sub-freezing air. Ember fell to her death as the jagged rocks frigid water finally claimed their black demon—the *Vagrant Shadow* finally found her eternal home....

Epilogue

In the following months to come after their expedition, Thomas went to serve his six months of jail time, he was later released three months early with a parole of twenty four month supervision. He would never forgot the "Vagrant Shadow" that rescued his brother from a certain death, and so, in honor of her life, Thomas started up a wild animal sanctuary where he would take in wounded wolves and other injured animals rehabilitate them back to health, and relocate them back into the wild. He called the operation *Feral Nation*.

Flora and Gene got married, but eventually became divorced within four years due to Gene's PTSD, and his violent and abusive impulses.

Tristan, Fang, Flame and the others lived their happy lives helping Thomas with Feral Nation teaching wolves in their own language how to be 'hunter aware'

after five years of physical therapy, and over $500,000 dollar surgery, Lesli Brenan was finally able to walk on her own, with the help of prosthetic legs.

Manny received capital punishment for treason, and since no one really wanted to bury a traitor, the government granted Thomas' permission to "throw his body to the wolves".

Brandon returned to Russia to study the Natives and their ways of life.

Sergeant Dawson got promoted to Command Officer for his act of valor.

Lesli and Thomas eventually got married after Thomas was finished with his parole. They later moved to California, where they would go to study Orca's in the wild. Orca's better known as 'wolves of the sea'

ABOUT THE AUTHOR

Daniel was born and raised in the Midwest. When he is not working as a C.N.A., he is often caught up in a visionary world of fantasy where most of his ideas stem from. On his free time Daniel loves to horseback ride, draw, bike ride, cook, pyrography, film directing, and go adventuring. He is the youngest of four siblings He currently resides in the United States but hopes to travel out west to one day open his café and riding stable along with a horse and cattle sanctuary for abused and neglected livestock. This is Daniel's first novella.